Confederate Ladies
OF RICHMOND

Susan Provost Beller

Twenty-First Century Books   Brookfield, Connecticut

This book is dedicated to the memory of
my husband's grandmother,
Josephine Lyons Murphy.
She would not have agreed with these
women's social and political views,
but she lived all ninety-nine years of her life
with the same indomitable spirit.

Cover photograph courtesy of Library of Congress

Photographs courtesy of The Library of Virginia: pp. 1, 24, 36, 38, 42, 51 (both), 58, 63, 64, 68, 73; The Virginia Historical Society: pp. 5 (far left), 20, 44, 61; The Museum of the Confederacy, Richmond, Virginia: pp. 5 (left middle, center left, far right), 14 (Katherine Wetzel), 15 (Katherine Wetzel), 21, 32 (Library of Congress), 46 (left, Katherine Wetzel), 47 (Library of Congress), 53 (Katherine Wetzel), 56 (Katherine Wetzel), 69 (bottom), 75 (Library of Congress), 84 (Katherine Wetzel), 85 (National Archives); Library of Congress: pp. 5 (center right), 19, 27, 30, 41, 66, 69 (top), 72; Culver Pictures: pp. 5 (right middle), 25, 31, 35, 81; Valentine Museum: pp. 8 (Cook Collection), 78; North Wind Picture Archives: p. 12

Library of Congress Cataloging-in-Publication Data
Beller, Susan Provost, 1949–
Confederate ladies of Richmond/Susan Provost Beller.
p.   cm.
Includes bibliographical references and index.
Summary: Tells stories of several Confederate women who supported the secession of the southern states during the Civil War, with particular emphasis on the seige of Richmond.
ISBN 0-7613-1470-9 (lib. bdg.)
1. Richmond (Va.)—History—Civil War, 1861–1865—Juvenile literature.   2. Richmond (Va.)—History—Civil War, 1861–1865—Women—Juvenile literature.   3. Women—Virginia—Richmond—History—19th century—Juvenile literature.   4. United States—History—Civil War, 1861–1865—Women—Juvenile literature.   [1. Richmond (Va.)—History—Civil War, 1861–1865—Women.   2. United States—History—Civil War, 1861–1865—Women.   3. Women—History—19th century.]   I. Title.
F234.R557B45   1999
973.7'082'09755451—DC21   98-42412   CIP   AC   Rev.

Published by Twenty-First Century Books
A Division of The Millbrook Press, Inc.
2 Old New Milford Road, Brookfield, Connecticut 06804
Visit us at our Web site: http://www.millbrookpress.com

ACKNOWLEDGMENTS

Several libraries have contributed to the researching and writing of this manuscript through their diligence in collecting both printed and manuscript materials of the Civil War. My thanks to the wonderful people at the Eleanor S. Brockenbrough Library of the Museum of the Confederacy; the Manuscripts Division, Periodicals, Rare Books, and Reading Rooms at the Library of Congress; the Special Collections Department at Alderman Library at the University of Virginia; and the Special Collections Department of Bailey-Howe Library at the University of Vermont. I am always deeply impressed with the welcoming response of librarians to my endless requests for information, and grateful for their assistance in accessing the exceptional materials they hold in their rare books and/or manuscript collections.

My thanks also to my daughter, Jennie, for some valuable comments when the manuscript was almost two-thirds complete, even though her observations led to a major rewrite!

As always with my books, my deepest thanks go to my husband, Michael, for always being willing to share both his enthusiasm and his encyclopedic knowledge of the Civil War, and also for his meticulous attention to my grammatical usage and syntax (for which I seldom thank him at the time).

CONTENTS

The Marriage of Hetty Cary

The date was January 19, 1865. The city of Richmond, Virginia, had now been a target of the Union army for over three years. The Confederacy was only three months away from the surrender that would end this horrible conflict—the Civil War. But in this almost beaten city there was a moment of joy, something that would be known as the social event of the war. Brigadier General John Pegram was home from the war for a very special occasion, his marriage to Hetty Cary.

The society of Richmond flocked to see this marriage. Hetty's cousin, Constance Cary, described the bride as "one called by many the most beautiful woman of the South," and the groom as "a son of Richmond universally honored and beloved." But the people gathered at the church had a very long wait. Varina Davis, wife of the President of the Confederate States of America, had arranged for the bride to ride in the Davis's private carriage. Strangely, the team of horses "had reared violently, refusing to go forward, and could not be controlled, so that they had been forced to get out of the carriage." Finally Hetty had no choice but to travel to the church in an old wagon.

St. Paul's Episcopal Church in Richmond survived the siege. It was here that Hetty Cary, a prominent member of Richmond society, married John Pegram in January 1865.

It was the second bit of bad luck to befall the bride, and Constance couldn't help but be concerned. Two days earlier, Hetty had visited her to show her the bridal veil she would be wearing. Constance wrote later, "As she turned from the mirror to salute us with a charming blush and smile, the mirror fell and was broken to small fragments, an accident afterward spoken of by the superstitious as one of a strange series of ominous happenings."

There would be another bad omen at the wedding itself. When Hetty began her march down the aisle, she dropped her handkerchief. As she bent to pick it up, she tore "the tulle veil over her face to almost its full length."[1] The wedding continued without further problems. Dr. Charles Minnegerode conducted the happy ceremony. After the wedding, the society of Richmond congratulated the bride and groom at a small reception. As diarist Judith McGuire recorded: "All was bright and beautiful. Happiness beamed from every eye."[2] Constance and other relatives "crowded around the couple, wishing them the best happiness our loving hearts could picture,"[3] in Constance's words.

The new bride returned with her husband to his quarters in Petersburg. On February 5, "while encouraging his men," according to the newspaper announcement, the twenty-two-year-old Pegram was killed. He was remembered and honored by a resolution of the Virginia General Assembly. Mr. Robertson of that body spoke of this "gallant warrior" who "in the aisle of a neighboring Church, lay, in his bier . . . just fallen in his country's defense."[4] No one wanted to be the one to tell his new bride of her loss. Captain Gordon McCabe wrote to Constance Cary, telling her of Pegram's death and its aftermath: "Our guns pulled past the ambulance where she [Hetty] was carding lint and I heard her laughing merrily within. I knew he was dead . . . while she sat there waiting for him to come to her." Instead of telling her, "word was sent to her that . . . it would be late before he could get back."[5] She returned to their home and slept that night, not knowing of her husband's death. Finally the next morning, some-one brought her to her husband's body, and that is how she found out what had happened.

Judith McGuire wrote: "Again has St. Paul's, his own beloved church, been opened to receive the soldier and his bride—the one coffined for a hero's grave, the other, pale and trembling, though still by his side, in widow's garb."[6] Hetty Cary Pegram walked down the aisle following her husband's coffin "crossed with a victor's palms besides his soldier's accoutrements."

Constance Cary rode to the cemetery in the carriage with the widow. She later wrote: "Snow lay white on the hill-sides, the bare trees stretched their arms above us, the river kept up its ceaseless rush and tumble, so much a part of daily life in our four years of ordeal that we had grown accustomed to interpret its voice according to our joy or grief."[7] Richmond again mourned a favorite son and Richmond's women expressed their grief in their diaries.

The experiences of these women who would record life in Richmond during the Civil War would not be the experiences of all or even a large part of the people living there at the time. The diarists were the "ladies"—educated women of the upper classes of Southern society. We can look back at them now and be shocked at what they believed about slavery and about the rights of people who were poorer than they and had a different color skin than they did.

But we can also look back and see them as the other soldiers of the Confederacy—the ones who fought their battles on the homefront. We have come to respect the Southern soldier even if we don't agree with the cause he was fighting for. We respect that he fought for what he believed in and lost all he believed in when the South lost the war. The same is true for these "ladies" of Richmond. Their opinions and their prejudices against the poor—white and black, free and slave—of the South may be shocking. But their courage and their willingness to fight for what they believed in make theirs a story worth telling.

And now, that story . . .

CHAPTER 1

Richmond at the Beginning

Richmond, as seen from the hill, with the James River flowing by, its broad level streets, full foliaged trees, and spacious homes, is a beautiful city. Rich in historic association, never did it appear more attractive to Southern eyes than when, arriving in the late autumn of '61, we found our Confederate Government established there, and the air full of activity."[1] Virginia Clay describes a Richmond soon to be lost in the horrors of the four years of the Civil War. By the end, Richmond would be a smoking ruin, its industrial district burned, its social order changed forever—a far cry from the city of 1860.

As the Civil War opened in 1861, Richmond was a prosperous city known for its beauty and its cultured society. The 1860 Census had counted just under 38,000 people in residence there. A new hotel, the Spotswood, had just opened at Eighth and Main Streets. The city had been visited by the Prince of Wales (later King Edward VII of Great Britain) in October 1860, and Richmond society had given him a magnificent welcome.

William Asbury Christian, in his detailed history of the city, called it "unusually prosperous" in 1860, with much building being done and more planned for the future. He told of the great exhibition of the city's first steam fire-engine that "could throw a stream of water over the American Hotel."[2] The city was planning a street railway system with horse-drawn cars to run from the Rocketts to Brook Road. The Tredegar Iron Works

A view of High Street in Richmond in 1862

was busy meeting the demand for new locomotives. Virginia as a whole was still mostly rural, with many large plantations. But it was also the most industrial state in the South and had the greatest population. Richmond, the capital of Virginia, was the South's third largest city.

Many of the people whose names would become famous in the Confederate Government were prominent in the United States Government in Washington, D.C., in 1860. But the election of Abraham Lincoln as President of the United States changed all that. On January 21, 1861, Virginia Clay sat in the balcony of the United States Senate and watched her husband, the Senator from Alabama, "take his portfolio under his arm and leave . . . in company with other no less earnest Southern Senators." Senator James Chesnut of South Carolina was the first to rise and speak. Virginia Clay remembered this, in spite of all that would happen ahead, as "the saddest day of my life."[3] She recalled: "As each Senator, speaking for his State, concluded his solemn renunciation of allegiance to the United States, women grew hysterical and waved their handker-chiefs, encouraging them with cries of sympathy and admiration."[4] Senator Clement Clay would become an ambassador for the new Confederate States of America and would end this war a prisoner, along with his friend Jefferson Davis, charged with treason against the United States they had once served together.

Jefferson Davis, the U.S. Senator from Mississippi, was among the senators who walked out on that momentous day. He would soon be elected as the first and only President of the Confederate States of America. Senator James Chesnut, who led the speeches that day, would become an aide to Jefferson Davis. His wife, Mary Boykin Chesnut, was a close friend of Varina Howell Davis, and would write a gossipy, insider's account of life at the highest political levels during the years the Confederacy was in existence.

South Carolina, Mississippi, Florida, Alabama, Georgia, Louisiana, and Texas all ended their association with the United States together. A month later delegates from these states met in Montgomery, Alabama, and formed the Confederate States of America. Everyone waited tensely to

Virginia Clay Clopton, shown here in later years, was the wife of U.S. Senator Clement Clay of Alabama. On January 21, 1861, he withdrew his state's support for the United States and joined the Confederate States of America.

see if Abraham Lincoln would allow them to secede peacefully and grant President Jefferson Davis's inaugural wish that they "not be obstructed by hostile opposition to our enjoyment of the separate existence and independence which we have asserted, and . . . intend to maintain."[5] The Southern border states, including Virginia, watched to see how Lincoln would react before making a decision about their own secession from the United States.

But peace was not to be possible. On April 12, 1861, with the Confederate siege of Fort Sumter in Charleston, South Carolina, the Civil War began. Virginia, North Carolina, Tennessee, and Arkansas voted to join the other Confederate States. For the women of Virginia in general, and Richmond in particular, it was not a moment too soon. Richmond resident Sarah (Sallie) Brock Putnam remembered: "It was at this period that the women of Virginia, and especially of Richmond, began to play the important part in public affairs, which they sustained with unflinching energy during four years of sanguinary [bloody] and devastating war." As she noted, "long before the ordinance of secession was passed by the Convention, almost every woman in Richmond had in her possession, a Confederate flag."[6] The women of Richmond were ready.

Judith McGuire, still living in her home in Alexandria, Virginia, across the Potomac River from the Union capital at Washington, D.C., knew that she would lose her home if Virginia seceded. But this knowledge did not discourage her feelings for the Southern cause: "I, who so dearly loved this Union, who from my cradle was taught to revere it, now most earnestly hope that the voice of Virginia may give no uncertain sound; that she may leave it with a shout."[7]

Kate Mason Rowland was a descendant of a signer of the Declaration of Independence. She was another Alexandria resident who would shortly find herself a refugee. Kate Rowland felt equally strongly about the duty owed to Virginia and the South by its residents. She copied into her diary, with great approval, parts of a letter that an aunt had sent: "It delights me to find you so true to the

Kate Mason Rowland lost her home when the Union army occupied Alexandria, Virginia, early in the Civil War.

Old Dominion, the Mother of us all . . . A true Son of Virginia labors to be worthy of the State which has given to the world so many great men."[8]

Phoebe Yates Pember was not surprised at the strong reaction of Southern women when the moment of crisis arrived: "The women of the South had been openly and violently rebellious from the moment they thought their states' rights touched. They incited the men to struggle in support of their views, and whether right or wrong, sustained them nobly to the end. They were the first to rebel—the last to succumb."[9]

As great as their support was for the Southern cause, many Southern women never believed that secession would lead to war. The Southerners were sure that the Union would let them go rather than put both nations through a fight. Judith McGuire, evicted from her home two days after the Virginia secession vote when the Union army occupied Alexandria, still did not believe that "Northern gentlemen . . . will engage in this . . . war of invasion."[10]

Robert E. Lee, an officer in the U.S. Army but a resident of Arlington, Virginia, turned down the offer to lead the Union armies and headed south to offer his services to defend his home state. His wife traveled with Judith McGuire for several days as they began the life as refugees that would lead both to spend the war in Richmond. McGuire found "Mrs. General Lee" to "have no doubt of our success."[11] Myrta Lockett Avary wrote years later of the feelings in that early period of the war: "They believed, as they hoped, that something would be done to prevent war. . . . We did not, we would not believe that brothers could war with brothers."

Avary was also not alone in believing that even if war came, it would be short: "Still we befooled ourselves. There would be a brief campaign, victory, and peace."[12] Sallie Putnam found among her friends the same optimism: "Sanguine expectations of speedy success were entertained."[13]

But war was coming, and the eleven states of the Confederate States of America made a fateful decision to move their capital to Richmond, Virginia. For the people of Richmond, who would be the target of Union offensives for the next four years, life would never be the same.

CHAPTER 2

The New Capital

"With the incoming of the Confederate Government, Richmond was flooded with pernicious [wicked] characters. The population was very soon doubled. Speculators, gamblers, and bad characters of every grade flocked to the capital. . . . Thieving, garrotting, and murdering were the nightly employments of the villains who prowled around the city," wrote Sallie Putnam.[1] Although there were severe changes as Richmond became accustomed to being the capital of the Confederacy, very few would agree with Mrs. Putnam's utter disgust with the "new" people coming to Richmond.

Richmond society was very rigidly organized as the war began. The city had a very active group of "society people," people who were wealthy and whose families were some of the oldest in Virginia. They were in power in Virginia and were also those who kept diaries and wrote the memoirs that give us a picture of life in Richmond at the time. There was also a large merchant class, some of whom were also quite wealthy.

But there were two other populations, much larger than Richmond "society" and the merchant class, and much poorer. These were the Richmond workers and the slaves. The workers were white and needed steady employment and a stable society to make even a meager living for their families. They worked mostly as laborers in the iron works and other industries, or as artisans, or on farms. The slaves were black and almost totally ignored in the writings of Richmond residents.

Their role as servants and plantation workers was simply taken for granted by the other classes in Richmond. These four groups of people all knew their place in the Richmond social structure and lived together in relative harmony before the chaos of the Civil War changed all these social relationships forever.

In fact, the first changes in Richmond as it became a capital city were usually considered to be good ones. The initial excitement and support for the "Cause" was shared among all of the people of Richmond, rich or poor, except, of course, many of the slaves. Richmond's residents were proud to have their city become the home of the new Confederacy. The spirits of Richmond society were lifted as the people welcomed President Davis and his wife. A home was provided for the Davis family. To Judith McGuire's delight, the home chosen was the home in which she had grown up. "I feel proud," she wrote, "to have those dear old rooms, arousing as they do many associations of my childhood and youth, filled with the great, the noble, the *fair* of our land . . ."[2]

Varina Davis was happy with her new home: "One felt here the pleasant sense of being in the home of a cultivated, liberal, fine gentleman." She admired the rooms, the fireplaces, and especially the garden. She also appreciated the warm welcome she received from the citizens of Richmond, speaking of the kindness of a neighbor who, when "our children were ill, she came full of hope . . . to cheer us by her good sense and womanly tenderness." Varina Davis was most "impressed by the simplicity and sincerity of their [Richmond ladies] manners." She found them "economical" and "full of enthusiasm . . . to promote the good of their families or their country."

Varina Davis did notice that some of the ladies of Richmond felt "that an inundation of people perhaps of doubtful standards . . . had poured over the city" but she was happy to see that even so, the society of Richmond "proffered a large hospitality."[3]

In addition to the government officials arriving to conduct their business, another large group of new residents were the refugees who had been

Jefferson and Varina Davis early in their marriage. Jefferson Davis was born in Kentucky the year before Lincoln. He attended West Point and later became a senator from Mississippi. He was elected president of the Confederacy on February 8, 1861.

evicted from their homes in northern Virginia by the Union army. Sallie Putnam noted that Richmond was becoming a "city of refuge. . . . The usual hotel and boarding-house accommodations were found altogether insufficient to supply comfortable places of sojourn for the great numbers demanding sympathy and shelter."[4]

Mrs. Robert E. Lee was one of the refugees, as was Mrs. John McGuire. Judith McGuire's husband, an Episcopalian minister, ran a school in Alexandria, Virginia, before the war. Too old to travel with the army as a chaplain, he became a clerk in the Post Office Department when the couple arrived in Richmond. Mrs. Lee had a home on

The Richmond home provided for the Davis family was Judith McGuire's childhood home. She and her husband came to Richmond as refugees from Alexandria.

Franklin Street. The McGuires' experience was more typical of that of the average refugee. Judith McGuire's diary records her increasingly desperate search for housing in Richmond, where "I do not believe there is a vacant spot in the city."[5] She finally did find a room to rent, although she would have to change residences several times before the war ended. Many were not so fortunate.

Many of the women whose diaries and memoirs are available to us spent only part of the war in Richmond, even if their husbands were there all the time. The wife of Senator Clement Clay was in Richmond early in the war. She returned for short periods of time during the war, but spent most of her time staying with various friends and relations after her home in Huntsville, Alabama, was taken by Union troops in 1862. She is very typical of the women who just could not afford to stay in Richmond, or who found life safer away from the capital, which was periodically under siege by Union forces.

Sara Pryor also spent the early part of the war in Richmond. Late in 1862, she joined her husband, Brigadier General Roger Pryor, at his camp. She was living in Petersburg, south of Richmond, when that city fell to the Union army in April 1865. She kept up a correspondence with friends in Richmond, especially a friend identified only as Agnes. In that way she could find out what was happening in Richmond during her absence.

Fannie A. Beers spent the early part of the war in Richmond, caring for sick and wounded soldiers. Later, she left the city and brought her nursing experience to other, less adequate hospitals. Even Mary Boykin Chesnut, close friend of Varina Davis, whose diary is probably the most famous woman's record of the Civil War era, did not stay in Richmond for the entire war. When her husband became the first of the Southern senators to resign, she followed him to Montgomery, Alabama, where

Mary Boykin Chesnut kept an extensive diary of Civil War events. Her diaries play an important role in understanding the effect the war had on everyday life in Southern society.

he helped to form the new Confederacy. When he went to Richmond as a Confederate Senator from South Carolina, she was delighted to join him there. But his career kept him in and out of Richmond. This annoyed Mary because she loved being in Richmond. She had great ambitions for her husband and saw him as part of the all-powerful Confederate leadership. Her gossipy account of the war always seems more exciting and enthusiastic when she was writing in Richmond.

All the arrivals in Richmond caused disruption and change. It was difficult for this small city to suddenly find itself adding so many new residents. But the greatest and most disruptive changes did not come from the new government officials or even from the great number of refugees who arrived there. The real change and the real problems came with increasing numbers of soldiers arriving to be trained and provisioned.

Coping with the common soldier of the Confederate army and the people who followed him trying to use up his pay through gambling and drink—this was the change that Sallie Putnam and her friends found so difficult to get used to.

CHAPTER 3

Military Camp

Richmond welcomed the arriving soldiers and saw to their every need. The soldiers came into the city for five or six weeks of training and to receive their supplies before being sent to the battlefields to fight. The Confederate soldier became an object of devotion for the ladies of Richmond, both young and old. Fannie Beers remembered that "the evening drills at the camp-grounds were attended by hundreds of ladies. . . . Language is quite inadequate to express the feeling which then lived and had its being in the hearts of all Southern women towards the heroes who had risen up to defend the liberties of the South."[1]

Mary Boykin Chesnut noticed especially the enthusiasm of the young girls as they welcomed the soldiers. Not only in Richmond, but throughout the South, as she traveled she noted that "parties of girls came to every station simply to look at the troops passing."[2]

The local newspaper the *Richmond Daily Whig* commented on the fascination that the army held for the citizens of the city: "Crowds of ladies and gentlemen repair every afternoon to the 'Camp of Instruction' of the Virginia Volunteers, at the Hermitage Fair Grounds; to the encampment of the South Carolina Regiments . . . and to other places of military interest . . . to view the battalion drills and dress parades."[3] Camps were set up "wherever there is space and eligible ground" according to another article.[4] Mary Boykin Chesnut now saw the city as "The fairgrounds are as covered with

A group of Confederate soldiers from Richmond posed for this photograph just before the First Battle of Bull Run (Manassas), July 21, 1861. The Confederate victory in this battle gave the first hint that the South was not going to be defeated in a few months, as the North had expected.

tents, soldiers. . . . As one regiment moves off to the army, a fresh one from home comes to be mustered in and takes its place."[5] Richmond had become "a great military camp," according to William Asbury Christian, and "the sound of the drum and the fife was heard in all directions."[6]

Judith McGuire described "one great barracks" with "troops . . . assembling there from every part of the Confederacy, all determined to do their duty."[7] For the soldiers, joining up was a way to show their patriotism and their support for the Southern cause. For the women of Richmond, and actually for all the women left behind, the soldiers provided a chance for them to do something for the cause also. As Sara Pryor noted: "After the soldiers left, silence and anxiety fell upon the town like a pall. What should we do next?"[8]

The women rapidly found something to do next. "To be idle was torture," wrote Sara Pryor, "We women resolved ourselves into a sewing society."[9] The women could not go off to fight. They could, however, provide clothing, tents, and other supplies for the soldiers who would. Judith McGuire wrote

"Ladies assemble daily, by hundreds, at the various churches, for the purpose of sewing for the soldiers."[10] Ellen Mordecai, writing to her brother in June 1861, bragged about the accomplishments of the "ladies in town," especially of one group that "have made with their own hands 75 tents and are I am told proceeding to complete the 100 which they undertook."[11] Varina Davis praised Mrs. Robert E. Lee and her daughters for making "one hundred and ninety-six socks and gloves" in spite of Mrs. Lee's illness while "confined to her chair, a hopeless victim of rheumatism."[12]

Sallie Putnam was amazed at the changes she saw in the women she knew. "Those who had formerly devoted themselves to gaiety and fashionable amusements," she wrote, "found their only real pleasure in obedience to the demands made upon their time and talents, in providing proper habiliments [clothing] for the soldier . . . the devotee of ease, luxury and idle enjoyment, found herself transformed into the busy sempstress [seamstress]."[13] Mrs. Putnam was not the only one who noted this change. Thomas Cooper DeLeon

Northern and Southern women contributed to the war effort in various ways, such as sewing uniforms, making bandages, nursing the wounded, and working in munitions factories.

commented also on these young Southern girls "reared so tenderly that the winds of heaven might not visit them too roughly . . . scarcely permitted to lace their own slippers." He praised the fact that, when the need arose, "they sewed rough fabrics for rough men with their delicate hands . . . [and] dressed wounds with never a tremor or a flush of false modesty." [14]

The ladies of Richmond found other tasks to keep them busy when not sewing. Preparing the soldiers for battle also meant preparing supplies for those who would be wounded. The women scraped pieces of lint from cotton cloth and rolled the lint into cotton strips to make bandages. The *Daily Whig* even published directions on how to make bandages "to the best advantage and with the greatest economy." [15]

Participation in the Cause could be shared by women of all economic classes. While the society ladies spent their time sewing and making bandages, many poorer women made cartridges for the soldiers' rifles. Douglas S. Freeman wrote: "For every woman in Richmond who was willing to do dangerous manual work, the munitions plants offered regular employment." But unlike the ladies who sewed, these women placed themselves in danger with their aid to the Cause: "explosions sometimes occurred at the loading rooms. In the worst of these, a number of girls and women were killed." [16]

With troops training in Richmond, displaced people arriving to find homes, and Richmond society adapting to meet the demand for clothing and provisions for the soldiers, it is no surprise that Richmond would change. It is also no real surprise that much of the change would not be for the good. The change that occurred was not quite as bad as Sallie Putnam had described, but there were real problems. Mary Boykin Chesnut could write with amusement in August 1861 of someone from her home state of South Carolina who "rode his horse through the barroom of this hotel" and of "how he scattered people and things right and left." [17] One small incident like this could seem amusing. But as such incidents became more common, people became upset by them.

Southern women worked at the Tredegar Iron Works in Richmond, the largest industrial plant in the South.

The *Examiner* for June 28, 1861, reported a small grocery "invaded by a dashing and gallant band of soldiers, in search of . . . whiskey." Two months later, they reported that the county jail had reached its full capacity. The negative reports continued: reckless driving of heavy wagons in October 1861, a crackdown on gambling and barrooms in November, advice to the citizens of Richmond to lock their doors at night, something they had never had to do before.[18] Thomas Cooper DeLeon wrote of this gambling and drinking by men who, "cut off from home ties and home amusements; led the life of dumb beasts in camp."[19] He felt, however, that many of the complaints were exaggerated. "The wonder is not that so many yielded to the seductions of drinks and cards," he wrote, "but that there were so many who did not. . . . There was little general drunkenness, and gambling . . . was more the exception than the rule."[20]

Having an increased number of people in the city also caused food shortages and scarcity of other items. Early in the war, this was only a little taste of the real shortages that would come, but it was frightening for the people living in Richmond. It is important to remember that many of the difficulties came about because things were changing so fast. Accounts written of life in the Union capital, at Washington, talk of some of the same problems that the people in Richmond were having. Later on life would be much harder in Richmond than in Washington. At first, however, both cities were in a state of flux as the leaders of the armies on both sides tried to create a fighting force in time for the first battle.

It is important to remember an added factor that may have made things seem worse in Richmond. The very rigid society that existed there (and elsewhere) before the war couldn't react quickly to change. And many changes were necessary to prepare for war. The result was turmoil for Richmond, and most of all for the parts of its society that had lived very pampered lives before the war. On the whole, they responded well, taking on tasks that no one would have thought them capable of doing. But every once in a while in the diaries and memoirs, their real shock comes through. Sallie Putnam tells a story of the "impudence" of common Confederate soldiers talking to unmarried girls of high society. She is absolutely shocked that they would "forget" themselves and talk to someone so much better than they in society. "Why indeed! any man that wears a stripe on his pantaloons thinks he can speak to any lady!"[21]

CHAPTER 4

The Bloody War Begins

For all of the preparations that they thought they had made, neither the Union nor the Confederacy was ready for the results of the first major battle at Manassas, Virginia, on July 21, 1861. The *Examiner* on July 22, 1861, announced: "We know that a victory, such as never yet was won on American soil, has been gained by Southern manhood. We know that it was resolutely contested by the enemy and that a terrible loss of life has taken place. We know the names of some general officers who have fallen . . . of our brothers, sons, husbands, friends who were not titled with such office we know nothing now."[1]

There was real joy and celebration as the news of the victory reached Richmond. Fannie Beers remembered "the wild excitement which . . . throbbed and pulsated throughout the crowded capital. . . . In the general rejoicing the heavy price of victory was for a time unheeded."[2] For most people, however, mixed in with their joy was terrible worry—no one had expected that so many lives would be lost on either side. For some the good news came quickly. Mary Boykin Chesnut was visited by Varina Davis herself, who told her: "A great battle has been fought. . . . Your husband is all right. . . . I had no breathe to speak; she went on [reading from the paper in her hand] 'Dead and dying cover the field.'" For other friends, Varina Davis delivered bad news.

Mary Boykin Chesnut joined Mrs. Davis in attending the funeral of the husband of one of

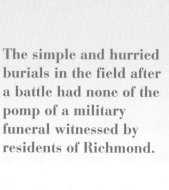

The simple and hurried burials in the field after a battle had none of the pomp of a military funeral witnessed by residents of Richmond.

their friends, the first of many. "Witnessed for the first time a military funeral. . . . The empty saddle and the led war-horse—we saw and heard it all, and now it seems we are never out of the sound of the Dead March. . . . It comes and it comes, until I feel inclined to close my ears and scream."[3]

Richmond was not ready for the wounded who were brought back to the city. Sallie Putnam wrote: "The condition of Richmond for the recep-

tion of the wounded was poor indeed. Our hospital accommodations at that time are scarcely worthy to be mentioned."[4] A citizen's group met on July 22 to plan for housing the wounded soldiers. The reporter for the *Richmond Daily Whig* noted that: "A large number of citizens came forward and proposed to receive the wounded into their homes . . . some proposing to take fifteen or twenty." All of these offers were accepted, but a deci-

Richmond was not prepared for the large numbers of wounded. Many had to be cared for in private homes, and the ladies quickly learned how to be nurses.

sion was also made to set up a hospital for the more seriously wounded. The proprietor of the St. Charles Hotel "tendered the use of the Hotel . . . without charge," noted the newspaper account.[5]

Care of the wounded could be arranged through use of private homes—all patriotic citizens seemed willing to do their part. But what about care of the Union prisoners, wounded or not? This issue caused much discussion around the city. Sallie Putnam indignantly wrote: "If our hospital accommodations for the sick and wound-

Libby Prison, converted from a tobacco warehouse, housed Union prisoners.

ed of our own armies were inadequate, we may surely be pardoned for not having comfortable accommodations for the prisoners." Several of those prisoners were housed for a time in tobacco warehouses that even Sallie Putnam admitted were "unfitted and insufficient in size." Libby Prison, a former tobacco warehouse, was soon opened to house the prisoners, and conditions improved somewhat.

Putnam hotly defended the South against claims of maltreatment of the prisoners saying that they received "the usual rations furnished the sick and wounded Confederates in the hospitals."[6] Phoebe Pember, who spent most of the war desperately attempting to find enough food for the wounded soldiers under her care at Chimborazo Hospital, also defended the South on this issue: "The Federal prisoners may have been starved at the South, we cannot deny the truth of the charge . . . but we starved with them."[7]

The topic of prisoner treatment was also discussed at the highest levels of society. Mary Boykin Chesnut was present at a dispute at a meeting of a ladies aid society. She wrote: "Mrs. Randolph proposed to divide everything sent us equally with the Yankee wounded and sick prisoners. . . . Some shrieked in wrath at the bare idea of putting our noble soldiers on a par with Yankees—living, dying, or dead. Fierce dames were some of them."[8]

Manassas taught both the North and the South that this would not be a quick, one-battle war. For the ladies of Richmond, struggling to care for their Southern heroes, this was just a bitter beginning to the long struggle. Many would have agreed with Judith McGuire's diary entry of July 23, 1861. She expressed her happiness at their victory and then added: "Oh, that they would now consent to leave our soil, and return to their own homes! . . . I do not desire vengeance upon them, but only that they would leave us in peace, to be forever and forever a separate people."[9]

CHAPTER 5

Feeling the War

"Strawberries are said to be more plentiful this season than has been known to be the case for many years. We suppose this fact is owing to the blockade . . . which prevents this luxury from finding its way to Northern ports,"[1] wrote the *Examiner* on June 1, 1861. The *Richmond Daily Whig* was reporting similar news, "prices have declined. . . . We may laugh at our enemies who think they can starve us into terms."[2] A few short months later it was their enemies who would laugh as the effect of the blockade began to be felt in Richmond. But for now the feeling of exultation and excitement was everywhere.

History books about the Civil War tell mostly of great battles, daring charges, and heroic stands by armies on the battlefield. A whole other war was fought in Richmond, the war against the Northern blockade of Southern ports. Not much is written about this war, and yet the decision to blockade the South—so that the Confederate government could not get war materials, medicines, food and other supplies from other countries— probably had as much to do with the South losing the war as any major battle did. At first the blockade brought excitement to the Southerners as the ladies defied the Union attempt to cut off outside supplies.

Hetty Cary began the war living in Baltimore, Maryland, a very Confederate city that happened to be located in the Union. She was ordered from the city for "shaking from the window of her father's home, while the Union troops marched by

The Northern blockade of Southern ports was devastating to the Confederacy. Running the blockade was dangerous but necessary to get arms and supplies to the South. Shown here are two blockade runners under full steam.

it, a Confederate banner smuggled through the lines," wrote her cousin, Constance Cary, with great excitement. Hetty was given the choice of going south or being arrested and imprisoned for her treasonous action. She chose to go south and her sister decided to leave with her. "The two sisters," Constance Cary bragged, used the opportunity to bring "drugs for the hospitals and uniforms for friends."[3]

Thomas Cooper DeLeon was amazed by the daring of the Southern girls in the early part of the war. Writing of the blockade runners, he said: "Some were the tenderest darlings of home and society, but they braved the roughness of camp and the long, icy rides to the river—often through hostile lines . . . to what was known as the 'Potomac Ferry.'" He claimed that Hetty and Constance Cary made several trips "bringing

Constance Cary (1843-1920) smuggled information and medicine to the South. Early in the war, she and her two cousins were at the center of Richmond society.

back rare drugs for the sick and information as valued for the generals." He noted that messages and plans were often smuggled in "curled in the soft tresses of a Baltimore woman, sent through as 'rebellious' on the flag of truce boat."[4] Constance Cary admitted to at least one smuggling expedition: "My one new evening dress of the war, bought in our raid on Washington [a trip she made with her mother] and sent through the lines by friends, had been reserved for the smartest party of the season."[5]

Sallie Putnam wrote, "These were the gala days of the war in Richmond. The dire realities, the sickness, the mutilation, the sufferings, the miseries, were yet unknown. Only the glory which might accrue was shadowed forth."[6]

Thomas Cooper DeLeon was amazed by the partying. "The younger and gayer people indulged in the 'danceable teas' . . . after their sewing-circles. . . . The result was a long season of more regular parties and unprecedented gaiety." DeLeon did mention that not everyone approved of the activity. Young himself at the time and enjoying these same parties, he commented on those who "frowned" this way: "These rigid Romans staid at home and worked on zealously in their manufacture of warm clothing, deformed socks and impossible gloves for the soldier boys." He admitted that "the young people had seized the society . . . and had run away with it for a brief space."[7] He described his fellow Richmonders as "hopeful, buoyant and sometimes giddy."[8]

Constance Cary was one of the young people enjoying the social life of Richmond to the fullest. Her cousins, Hetty and Jennie Cary, had come south from Baltimore, Maryland, and the three of them, known as the "Cary Invincibles," were at the center of Richmond society. They were thrilled when they were selected by the Confederate Congress "to make the first battle-flags of the Confederacy." Romantic historical accounts say that the girls made the flags from their own dresses because no material was available. Writing years later, Constance Cary, now Harrison, corrected these accounts: "It is certain we possessed no wearing apparel in the flamboyant hues of poppy red and vivid dark blue required."[9]

Material for new dresses or flag-making would be one of the first items missed as the blockade by the North began to be felt in Richmond. Sallie Putnam noted that "Cotton and woolen fabrics soon brought double prices."[10] What was interesting was that while the "staple articles," as Putnam called them, had become harder to find, many luxury items were still available, at reasonable prices. There were "rich silks, laces, etc., and the merchants, supposing there would be but little demand for such articles, were willing to sell at the usual prices, and even . . . at or below cost."[11] Only looking back, however, did the diarists realize that once these supplies were gone, no more would be brought in to take their place.

Food was still plentiful except for "imported items." Catherine Hopley, a British woman temporarily unable to return home because of the blockade, commented that "if the Northern Pres-

This 1868 market scene in Richmond is very different from the market at the start of the Civil War, when goods and produce were plentiful.

ident could take a peep at Richmond some fine day, he would think he had not yet made much progress."[12] What the people of Richmond were beginning to feel was the increase in prices as necessary goods began to become scarce. Sallie Putnam wrote of "extortion" in Richmond during the winter of 1861–1862. General John Henry Winder, in charge of provisions for the city, attempted to control how fast prices were rising. As a result, the merchants just hoarded their goods and refused to sell. Sallie Putnam complained about these "hucksters" who "charged what prices they pleased for their merchandise, and we were forced to pay them or abstain from many necessary articles of food altogether."[13]

Times were not really hard yet in comparison to what was to come. Any talk of these scarcities leading to actual defeat would have seemed laughable at this point. Parties were common since, as Virginia Clay noted, "there were heroes to dine and to cheer in Richmond."[14] Looking back, however, Clay wrote, "While few, I think, perceived it clearly at that early day, yet in the spring of '62 the fortunes of the Confederacy were declining."[15] The blockade was taking its toll. The "extortion" and shortages just beginning to be seen in Richmond would get worse.

CHAPTER 6

Under Attack

" The flashes of the guns are visible on the horizon, followed by the deep intonations of the mighty engines of destruction, echoing and reverberating from hill to hill. . . . Hundreds of men, women, and children were attracted to the heights around the city to behold the spectacle."[1] John B. Jones recorded the excitement of this attack on Richmond in June 1862, part of what is called the Seven Days Battle. Sara Pryor found it more horrible than exciting: "All the afternoon the dreadful guns shook the earth and thrilled our souls with horror. I shut myself in my darkened room. . . . Everyone had gone out to the hills to witness the aurora of death to which we were later to become so accustomed."[2]

Thomas Cooper DeLeon noted that "for the first time, the people of Richmond began to see the realities of war. When the firing began, many ladies were at work for the soldiers in the churches. These flocked to the doors, pale and anxious, but with a steady determination in their faces."[3] Richmond came under attack several times in the late spring of 1862. Both armies had spent the time after Manassas the preceding summer preparing their armies for the long fight ahead.

In spring the Union army came to Virginia in an attempt to take Richmond from the east by going up the peninsula between the James and the York rivers. The Peninsula Campaign brought an army of more than 100,000 Union soldiers to

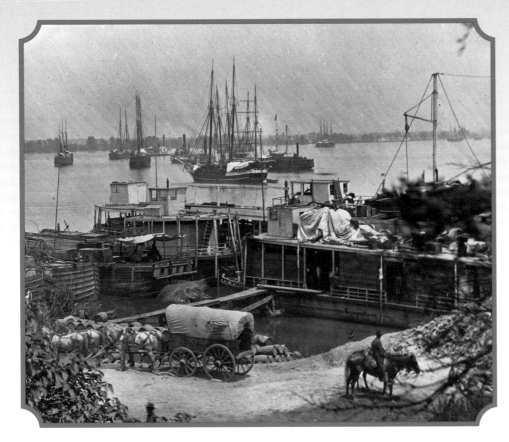

Federal boats unloaded at a dock in City Point, Virginia, to supply Union soldiers brought by boat to Virginia.

southern Virginia by boat from Washington. The soldiers were to fight their way up the peninsula to Richmond, located seventy-five miles away. There they intended to capture the Confederate capital and bring the war to a quick end—that, at least, was the plan developed by Major General George B. McClellan, the Union army comman-

der. This plan brought the fight close to Richmond at the Battle of Seven Pines on May 31 and June 1, 1862, and during the Seven Days Battle from June 25 to July 1. The fighting scared many of the people living in Richmond, and a large number left the city in early May. Judith McGuire described a "panic . . . lest the enemy should get

A Union battery is shown shelling an area close to Richmond
during the Seven Days Battle from June 25 to July 1, 1862.

to Richmond."[4] Sallie Putnam wrote that "Citizens were leaving by hundreds in all directions, and in all manner of conveyances. Baggage-wagons, heaped up with trunks, boxes and baskets, were constantly rattling through the streets."[5]

Even the Confederate Secretary of War, G. W. Randolph, had ordered the War Department records and papers packed up and removed in order to protect them in case the city were taken. He did add to his statement that "This is only intended as a prudent step. . . . There is no need, therefore, for any panic in the city . . . we have every reason to think that the city can be successfully defended."[6] Such an action did not encourage the people, even with his reassurance. Judith McGuire found it "distressing to see how many persons are leaving Richmond, apprehending that it is in danger." She refused to leave, saying "it will not—I know it will not—fall."[7]

Constance Cary, although admitting to being frightened herself, had nothing but praise for the Richmond residents who decided to stay: "The women left in Richmond had, with few exceptions, husbands, fathers, sons and brothers in the fight. I have never seen a finer exhibition of calm courage than they showed. . . . No one wept or moaned aloud. All went about their task of preparing for the wounded."[8] They would need their courage when the wounded and dead were brought in.

LaSalle Corbell Pickett, wife of Confederate General George E. Pickett, would remember "the long procession of wounded, nearly five thousand, young boys, middle-aged and white-haired men . . . suffering in every way; parched, feverish, agonized, wearing a look of mute agony no words may describe."[9] On June 27, Judith McGuire wrote: "The carnage is frightful." The next day she was forced to record the death of the son of a close friend: "Dearly have I loved that warm-hearted, high-minded, brave boy, since his early childhood."[10] LaSalle Corbell Pickett found it difficult to even go outside her home: "As you walked the streets some scene to make the heart ache would be enacted before your eyes. . . . From some wife, sister, or mother you heard words of

reported to be retreating. "The city is sad, because of the dead and dying, but our hearts are filled with gratitude and love. The end is not yet . . ."[12]

For many individual Richmond families, the fighting near Richmond had brought the end for someone they loved. Constance Cary remembered that "Day after day one heard the wailing dirge of military bands preceding a soldier's funeral. One could not number those sad pageants in our leafy streets; the coffin with its cap and sword and gloves, the riderless horse with empty boots in the stirrups of an army saddle!"[13]

Victory, for now, was theirs. But, as Sallie Putnam, busy with the care of the wounded, noted: "We had neither the time nor inclination to make merry over the triumphs of our arms."[14] A horrible lesson had been learned in Richmond according to LaSalle Corbell Pickett: "People realized with a sudden shock the actualities of internecine strife . . . . Before they had seen only its pride and pomp, and its martial showing. . . . It rendered them more determined, more earnest, more sincere."[15]

tenderest meaning, or bitterest weeping, or scream of agony as you passed along. . . . Black waved its sad signal from door to door."[11]

Finally, on June 30, Judith McGuire recorded the news she had been awaiting. General McClellan was

CHAPTER 7

Military Hospital

"I loved very dearly these heroes whom I served. . . . Every hour of toil brought its own rich reward. These were Confederate soldiers. God had permitted me to work for the holy cause. This was enough to flood my whole being with content and deepest gratitude."[1] Fannie Beers was not the only woman who found nursing the wounded soldiers to be her mission during the Civil War. But hers was one of the most moving statements of what this meant to her.

The women of Richmond who had supported the cause of the South with their sewing earlier in the war now turned to nursing in incredible numbers. From Manassas on, even when under fire themselves, these women continued to care for their heroes. They opened their homes to the wounded if they had room and visited and cared for the wounded at the various hospitals opened around the city. Louisa Triplett Harrison, growing up in Richmond during the Civil War, remembered that "in our house, as in many in Richmond, one large room was devoted to the sick and wounded soldiers. The cots were arranged as in a hospital, and filled again as soon as emptied. . . . My mother, as did many ladies, baked bread regularly twice a week for the Robinson Hospital, directly behind our house."[2]

Some of the Richmond nurses became famous for their work. Miss Sally Tompkins, known to all as "Aunt Sallie," was actually commissioned as an officer in the Confederate army in recognition of her hospital work. She opened her hospital at her

Captain Sally Tompkins (inset) established a hospital in 1862 in Richmond.

own expense after the Battle of Manassas and kept it open throughout the war. One writer remembered her as "original, old-fashioned and tireless in well doing . . . as resolute as a veteran."[3] Tompkins Hospital earned a reputation for the high quality of care given to its patients. It also had a reputation for fairness. Mary Boykin Chesnut tells a story of going around to hospitals seeking to visit with soldiers from South Carolina and to bring them gifts. Upon visiting Tompkins Hospital and asking after "Carolinians," Chesnut "was rebuked. I deserved it." Miss Tompkins told her: "'I never ask where the sick and wounded come from.'"[4]

The world's largest general military hospital was built on Chimborazo Heights in Richmond with eight thousand beds for wounded and sick

Chimborazo Hospital, seen here stretching across the horizon, was the largest general military hospital in the world. The buildings covered acres, and units were added as the war dragged on.

soldiers. Mrs. Phoebe Pember, a widow, was named "chief matron" of the huge hospital. In 1864 she became ill and was sent away for one month to recuperate. For her, leaving was terribly difficult: "It had been like tearing body and soul apart . . . to leave my hospital, from which I had never been separated but one day in nearly four years."[5] Phoebe Pember was known for her ability to organize materials to best care for the soldiers and known also for her "will of steel."

But her memoirs speak also of the pain she felt in doing her task, especially when faced with what she called the "hardest trial of my duty . . . telling a man in the prime of life, and the fullness of strength that there was no hope for him."[6] Phoebe Pember stayed with her sick and wounded beyond the end of the war. When the Union army finally captured Richmond and took over Chimborazo Hospital for their own soldiers, Pember saw to the relocation and care of all the remaining Confederate patients.

Sally Tompkins and Phoebe Pember are definitely the most famous of Richmond's nurses. But they are only two of the many devoted women who found their way to help the cause in the care of the wounded. Every diary, every memoir speaks of the devotion of the women of Richmond to their sick and wounded soldiers. Varina Davis wrote in her own memoirs that she was one of the few women in Richmond not involved in nursing the soldiers. Instead, she served as the agent for distributing money and gifts sent from other areas for use in the hospitals.

That experience brought her into a great number of home hospitals. She names several women whom she regularly saw working in an atmosphere "fetid with the festering wounds." She praised the many people who "bravely . . . bore aloft the old standard of Virginia hospitality."[7]

Sara Pryor remembered the horrible scene when the first casualties were shipped into an unprepared Richmond from the Battle of Manassas. "Every house was opened for the wounded. They lay on verandas, in halls, in drawing-rooms of stately mansions."[8] She herself decided to volunteer at the hospital set up in Kent & Paine's warehouse, but fainted from the sights and smells. She was horrified at failing this test and deter-mined to overcome her fear and faintness. Finally she achieved her goal of making herself tolerate the horrors of the hospital and joined the other women to do her share of the nursing.

Other Confederate women would have understood Sara Pryor's sense of shame and her determination to do her part. The women of Richmond began to see their work in the hospitals as a form of soldiering. For many of them, like Sara Pryor, it truly was a battle to be won over their own horror at the conditions in the hospitals, but their determination carried them through. Judith McGuire captured the utter devotion of the women in her diary entry of June 15, 1861. She wrote: "I do not believe there is a woman among us who would not give up every thing but the bare necessaries of life for the good of the cause." The women, she stressed, "think no effort, however self-sacrificing, is too great to be made for the soldiers."[9] The following year she would write again: "what can the ladies of Virginia ever do to compensate them [the soldiers] for all they have done and suffered for us?"[10]

CHAPTER 8

Hard Times

"My wife has obviated one of the difficulties of the blockade, by a substitute for coffee, which I like very well. It is simply *corn meal, toasted like coffee*. . . . It costs five or six cents per pound—coffee, $2.50," wrote John B. Jones in his diary.[1] His wife was not alone in creating substitutes for items increasingly scarce and expensive as the war continued. Sara Pryor learned some tricks from Mrs. Laighton, granddaughter of Patrick Henry, a Virginia Revolutionary War hero, and wrote excitedly about "the herb, 'life everlasting,' which . . . would make excellent yeast." She also borrowed Mrs. Laighton's recipe for coffee—"the best substitute for coffee was not the dried cubes of sweet potato, but parched corn or parched meal, making a nourishing drink."[2] Sallie Putnam found a successful tea recipe from "leaves of the currant, blackberry, willow, sage, and other vegetables."[3]

By 1863, the citizens of the South were suffering. The Union blockade was successfully cutting off supplies of the luxuries upon which the ladies of Richmond depended. They stubbornly and proudly invented substitutes for coffee, tea, and other food-related luxuries. But for many of the ladies, what they mourned most was the lack of beautiful clothes and other apparel. Sometimes it is hard to understand how these somewhat frivolous items could have been so critical to them. Reading the diaries, however, shows that, for some of them at least, having to do without their new clothes was the biggest sacrifice they made for the cause. Sara Pryor stated it most strongly: "I could starve with perfect serenity. I could live without the latest novel, the late magazines, eggshell china, rich attire, jewels; but I had not had a new bonnet for three years."[4] She arranged for someone to try to bring one through the blockade for her, but the man was caught and brought before her husband, Brigadier General Roger Pryor. Her husband confiscated the goods and she did not get her new bonnet after all.

Most ladies did not feel as strongly as Sara Pryor. Mrs. Mark Valentine wrote proudly of her homespun dress made from wool from her aunt's sheep: "She gathered wool and spun it into cloth and gave my sister and myself each a dress, which we made and wore with great pride over big hoop skirts. . . . I made a hat of the sleeve of an old broadcloth coat and put a feather in it."[5]

John B. Jones commented on the bonnet-making taking place in the summer of 1863: "Everywhere the ladies and children may be seen plaiting straw and making bonnets and hats. Mrs. Davis and the ladies of her household are fre-quently seen sitting on the front porch engaged in this employment."[6]

Judith McGuire, the most practical of all of the diarists, could comment on buying "a calico dress, for which I gave $2.50 per yard, and considered it a bargain." For her, what was most missed was writing paper: "The scarcity of blank-books, and the very high prices, make them unattainable to me; therefore I have determined to begin another volume of my Diary on some nice wrapping-paper [probably just brown paper] . . . though not very pleasant to write on, yet it is one of the least of my privations."[7]

The diaries and reminiscences all speak of their writer's sense of loss as things that had always been easily available to them slowly disap-peared. Most mourned their losses with "cheerful

At the beginning of the Civil War, Richmond society women wore elaborate dresses of silk and lace, as shown here on Hetty Cary Pegram (left). As basic goods became more and more scarce, dresses were often styled more simply and were made of wool, gingham, or whatever material could be found (right).

fortitude" as "brilliant examples of virtuous patriotism and heroic contentment," in Sallie Putnam's words.[8] But she also noted that it was some of the little things that were lacking that caused the most annoyance. She wrote of "a sad want of school books," since "books were the last consideration in that eccentric trade [blockade running]. Inconveniences arose at every step to impede the progress of education in the Confederacy."[9]

In the midst of this mourning over missing luxuries, there was more serious need in the city. While the wealthy ladies could sell off personal items, or buy goods smuggled in through the blockade, this was not possible for the poor, and as the war continued, hunger became a serious problem for them. William Asbury Christian notes that, "Provisions had gotten so scarce in the city that the poor could scarcely get food."[10] On April 2, 1863, "A mob, principally of women, appeared in the streets, attacking the stores. Their object seemed to be to get any thing they could; dry-goods, shoes, brooms, meat, glassware, jewelry,

were caught up by them. The military was called out," Judith McGuire recorded in her diary.[11]

It is hard to find out exactly what happened because this "Bread Riots" incident was kept very quiet, and the diaries and reminiscences give very different versions of the story. McGuire's account is the most complete. Apparently the governor of Virginia and President Jefferson Davis spoke to the protesting women at some point, expressing sympathy for the poor in the city. It appears also that the initial march was made up of women and children who genuinely were in need and simply wanted to make that known to the public officials. The group gradually was enlarged, however, by persons who used the occasion for general looting and disturbance. Whatever the true facts of the situation, the Confederate Secretary of War ordered that "nothing relative to the unfortunate disturbance which occurred in the city today . . . be sent over the telegraph lines in any direction for any purpose." The newspapers were also "advised" not to publish anything because the

There are differing accounts of the "Bread Riots" of April 2, 1863, in Richmond. But most agree that initially the marchers were mostly needy women and children.

facts were "liable to misrepresentation," and might "tend to embarrass our cause."[12]

The surviving accounts range from those that are understanding and sympathetic to the needs of the poor to ones that saw the event as a Union-inspired attempt to overthrow the government. Varina Davis wrote that her husband, President Davis, had concluded "that it was not bread they wanted, but that they were bent on nothing but plunder and wholesale robbery."[13] Sallie Putnam also wrote that, although there was real hunger among the poor in the city, "the sufferers for food were not to be found in this mob of vicious men and lawless viragoes [loud, demanding women]."[14] Kate Mason Rowland saw a conspiracy: "It was [a] shameful proceeding, probably instigated by the Yankees."[15]

Judith McGuire was more balanced in her account. She wrote that the riots began with "those who were really in want" but grew to include "the very worst class of women, and a great many who were not in want at all."[16] Sara

Pryor's friend Agnes wrote to her of seeing a "pale, emaciated girl, not more than eighteen . . . [revealing] a mere skeleton of an arm," who told her that the women were starving and "we are going to the bakeries and each of us will take a loaf of bread. That is little enough for the government to give us after it has taken all our men." [17]

Whatever actually happened, for the people of Richmond the Bread Riots, in Judith McGuire's words, "darkened the annals of Richmond." [18] But real scarcity and want were coming to Richmond. By the winter of 1864, these privations and scarcities of 1863 would come to be seen as just minor inconveniences.

CHAPTER 9

Coping With Death

"How can I record the sorrow which has befallen our country! General T. J. Jackson is no more. The good, the great, the glorious Stonewall Jackson is numbered with the dead," wrote Judith McGuire on May 12, 1863.[1] Death had become a part of the everyday life of Richmond by the third year of the war. So much so, that only the deaths of the most important people or of family members are recorded in the diaries. Early in the war, the death of everyone even slightly known was cause for comment. Now it took either a family loss or a severe loss to the Cause to merit mention in an account. The death of Stonewall Jackson brought universal grief to the people of Richmond because he had proven to be a brilliant general who had helped the Confederacy achieve its greatest victories.

Judith McGuire recorded that "Almost every lady . . . visited the [train] car, with a wreath or a cross of the most beautiful flowers, as a tribute. . . . The body lies in state to-day at the Capitol, wrapped in the Confederate flag, and literally covered with lilies of the valley and other beautiful Spring flowers."[2] Kate Mason Rowland visited the casket and wrote in her diary: "Only a thin glass lay between me and the gray, lifeless features of him who was our country's boast. The city is one house of mourning."[3] The *Examiner* reported, "Had a visible pall overspread the city, it would not have expressed grief more profound, nor sorrow more universal, than that which fired every heart, and sat

This is the published order of procession for the funeral of Lieutenant General Thomas Jonathan "Stonewall" Jackson. He was wounded accidentally by his own men on May 2, 1863, during the Battle of Chancellorsville and died on May 10.

upon every countenance. It was as though death had come home to every household, and snatched the one dearest away."[4]

All businesses closed down, and the entire route of the funeral procession was crowded with weeping people. Stonewall Jackson was given the largest funeral ever held in Richmond. A grieving Sallie Putnam wrote that "the tower of strength upon which we had leaned had been overthrown."[5] Only the death of Robert E. Lee could have caused more pain to the people of Richmond. Sara Pryor noted how universal the grief was: "By every man, woman, and child in the Confederacy this good man and great general was mourned as never man was mourned before."[6]

About a year later, there was a different and less significant public death when Joe, the five-year-old son of President and Mrs. Davis, fell to his death from the back porch of the Confederate White House. Although a personal loss for the Davises and for others, such as his godmother Virginia Tunstall Clay, what is surprising is that the memoirs show he was also mourned by the entire city. Judith

ORDER OF THE PROCESSION
AT THE FUNERAL OF
LIEUT. GEN. T. J. JACKSON.

1st. Military
2d. Pall Bearers. }BODY.{ Pall Bearers.
3d. Family of the deceased.
4th. Faculty of the Va. Military Institute.
  Officers "   "   "   "
  Members of the Quartermaster Dep't.
  "   "   " Subsistence   "
  Servants of the Va. Military Institute.
5th. Elders of the Lex'n. Presbyterian Church.
6th. Deacons of the Lexington Pres. Church.
7th. Reverend Clergy.
8th. Trustees, Professors and Students of Washington College.
9th. Franklin Society.
10th. Town Council.
11th. County Magistrates.
12th. Members of the Bar and Medical Profession.
13th. Officers and Soldiers of the Confederate Army.
14th. Bible Society.
15th. Sabbath Schools.
16th. Citizens.
The Procession will be formed at the V. M. I. at 10 o'clock, A. M., on Saturday, the 16th inst.
The body will lie in state at the V. M. I. during Friday.   FRANCIS H. SMITH,
  V. M. I., May 10th, 1863.   Superintendent.

McGuire wrote movingly in her diary of the news and said that the Davises "have the deep sympathy of the community."[7] Constance Cary wrote of "the mother's passionate grief and the terrible self-control of the President." She also noted, with some surprise, that "To the bier of the little lad, it seems that every child in Richmond brought flowers."[8]

Two weeks later came the burial of another famous general, J.E.B. Stuart, Lee's renowned cavalry commander. Again "the church was . . . crowded with citizens" along with "President Davis, General Bragg, General Ransom, and other civil and military officials in Richmond."[9] Judith McGuire wrote of her own distress at not being able to attend: "The funeral took place this evening. . . . My duty to the living prevented my attending it, for which I am very sorry; but I was in the hospital from three o'clock until eight, soothing the sufferers in the only way I could . . . [and] others of our household were at the funeral."[10]

In the midst of the news of official deaths come the personal stories of deaths of family members, often heart-breaking to read about. Cornelia Peake McDonald lived in Winchester, Virginia, during the Civil War. Her husband was wounded and taken prisoner in the fall of 1864. Eventually he was sent home in a wounded prisoner exchange and brought to Richmond. Mrs. McDonald traveled by train to the home of friends in Richmond so that she could bring her convalescing husband home to Winchester. "I sat all day happy, talking and laughing with friends, and joyfully anticipating my arrival at Richmond." On arrival she found people unusually quiet. Puzzled, she entered the house and "Mrs. Holliday . . . pointed to an open door. . . . I went, and the object I first saw was my husband's corpse, stretched on a white bed. . . . That same night I heard of the death of my dear sister Lizzy."[11]

Judith McGuire recorded a list of dead she knew from the soldiers who fought at the Battle of Gettysburg, commenting on her memories of them. Then she added: "But trying as it is to record the death of those dear boys, it is harder still to speak of those of our own house and blood . . . our nephew, the bright, fair-haired boy, from

Wagons carried the wounded soldiers after the Battle of Gettysburg, July 1-3, 1863. The battle was costly for both the North and South—casualties numbered 22,000 for the North and just slightly more for the South.

whom we parted last summer . . . is among the dead at Gettysburg."[12] Mary Boykin Chesnut recorded an especially sad story of the death of a friend at the Battle of Antietam in September 1862. His son was wounded and captured in the same battle. His wife was at home, coping with the recent death of their daughter. The wife, hearing of her husband's death, still ill herself, died. Wrote Chesnut, "These are sad, unfortunate memories. Let us run away from them."[13]

William Asbury Christian had written of the spirit of the citizens of Richmond early in the war: "An invincible determination had been formed that if the flow of blood could not stop the invading hosts, the ashes of a great city would be the monument left to them. Nothing was too dear to sacrifice for the sake of the great cause."[14] The *Richmond Daily Dispatch* wrote, "Should the Abolitionists advance on Richmond, as they have threatened, the ladies may have their hands full; for our citizens, to a man, will die in the ditch rather than see the streets of Richmond polluted by the tread of the Abolition foe."[15]

But the women diarists were beginning to reach their limit. After a long and futile search for a wounded cousin, while seeing "men in every stage of mutilation," Constance Cary recorded an almost unpatriotic thought for a Confederate woman to be thinking. In spite of her love for the Cause, she wrote, "The impression of that day was ineffaceable. It left me permanently convinced that nothing is worth war!"[16]

CHAPTER 10

The End Nears

By the autumn of 1864 the Southern States found themselves ravaged of everything either edible or wearable. . . . For nearly three years the blockade of our ports and frontier had made the purchase of anything really needful, impracticable," wrote Virginia Clay.[1] The end was coming. It was now inevitable. But the people of Richmond were determined to not show any despair. Sara Pryor wrote about the "starvation parties," so called "on account of the absence of refreshments impossible to be obtained. . . . I think all who remember the dark days of the winter of 1864–1865 will bear witness to the unwritten law enforcing cheerfulness. It was tacitly understood that we must make no moan, yield to no outward expression of despondency or despair."[2]

John B. Jones, recording his daily entry for March 18, 1864, wrote: "My daughter's cat is staggering to-day, for want of animal food. Sometimes I fancy I stagger myself. We do not average two ounces of meat daily; and some do not get any for several days together."[3] Mrs. Mark Valentine remembered meals of "bread, a dish of rice, and no butter."[4] Sallie Putnam wrote: "In Richmond we had never known such a scarcity of food—such absolute want of the necessaries of life. . . . Our markets presented a most impoverished aspect."[5]

By the late summer of 1864 the price of food items in Richmond had reached incredible heights. Flour that had seemed incredibly costly at $100 a barrel a year earlier was now $400 a barrel. Butter was $8 per pound. In April, Judith

at $10 per pound. White sugar is not to be thought of by persons of moderate means."

By August the situation would be worse. McGuire's diary entry for August 22 opens with "Just been on a shopping expedition for my sister and niece, and spent $1,500 in about an hour . . . $5 apiece for spools of cotton [thread]; $5 for a paper of pins, etc. It would be utterly absurd, except that it is melancholy to see our currency depreciating so rapidly."[6] The City Council "appropriated $30,000 for relief of the poor to keep them from starvation."[7] John B. Jones, working in the War Department, knew better than most the actual situation in Richmond. He wrote that "the population of the city is not less than 100,000, and the markets cannot subsist 70,000."[8]

Richmond was well beyond the limits of what could have been supported in the best of times, and the conditions were the worst in its history. At one point Jones recorded in his diary: "The prisoners on Belle Isle (8000) have had no meat for eleven days. The Secretary says the Commissary-

McGuire, now earning $125 a month as a clerk in the Commissary Department, wrote, "Groceries are extremely high. We were fortunate in buying ten pounds of tea, when it only sold for $22 per pound. Coffee now sells for $12, and brown sugar

General informs him that they fare as well as our armies, and so he refused . . . a permit to buy and bring to the city cattle he might be able to find."[9]

Food was not the only scarce item. The ladies of Richmond, who mourned their loss of luxury wearing apparel a year or two earlier, now could not even find more common material. Judith McGuire found herself a new "occupation" in January 1864—shoemaker: "I am busy upon the second pair of gaiter boots. They are made of canvas, presented me by a friend . . . cut out by a shoemaker, stitched and bound by the ladies, then soled by a shoemaker for the moderate sum of fifty dollars."[10]

Virginia Clay also found herself busy trying to create necessary items from old materials at hand. "Every scrap of old leather from furniture, trunk, belt or saddle was saved for the manufacture of rough shoes," she wrote. She was living on "potato coffee and peanut chocolate," and happy to have even that. "Needles," she wrote, "were becoming as precious as heirlooms; pins were the rarest of luxuries." She was writing her letters on pieces of wallpaper and sometimes had to make her own "writing fluids" from berries.[11]

Myrta Lockett Avary recounted a visit to a country home where "there was plenty to eat. . . . I always remember that fact . . . because it was beginning to be so pleasant and unusual to have enough to eat. . . . How often we were hungry! and how anxious and miserable we were!"[12]

In the midst of the misery there were some who never lacked for anything during the course of the war. These people, many of whom made money by smuggling goods through the blockade and by speculating, were an embarrassment to many of the old-time families of Richmond. Many of the diarists refer to them in passing, but Judith McGuire wrote about them with great feeling in her diary entry of January 8, 1865: "In the midst of the wounded and dying, the low state of the commissariat [food storage warehouses], the anxiety of the whole country, the troubles of every kind by which we are surrounded, I am mortified to say that there are gay parties . . . where the most elegant suppers are served—cakes, jellies,

Blockade-runner ships were built for speed. Some unscrupulous owners and captains became wealthy by supplying high-priced goods to the few who could afford them.

ices in profusion, and meats of the finest kinds in abundance. . . . I passed a house where there was music and dancing. The revulsion of feeling was sickening." [13]

Even Sara Pryor, who had tolerated blockade-running earlier in the war, had no patience with it as times became harder and agreed with her friend Agnes, who wrote, "There is not a bonnet for sale in Richmond. Some of the girls smuggle them, which I for one consider in the worse possible taste, to say the least. We have no right at this time to dress better than our neighbors, and besides, the soldiers need every cent of our money." [14] Although others only hint at the people who lived well in the midst of the starving city, many others had also noticed. John S. Wise wrote discreetly of the blockade runners who "alone seemed possessors of the secret wherewith, even amidst poverty and want, to conjure up wealth and luxury." [15]

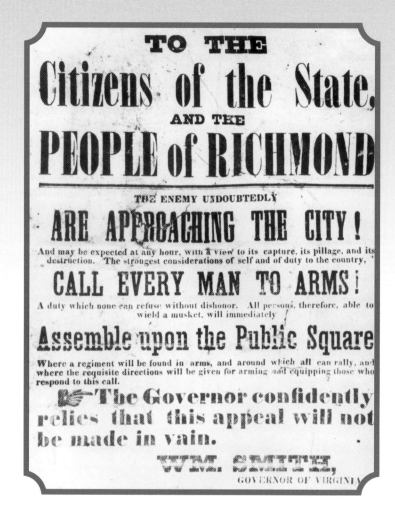

For most of Richmond, however, the social life that winter of 1864–1865 was indeed "starvation parties" with no refreshment "save the amber-hued water from the classic James" [River].[16] People met and put on plays and "tableaux." Life went on in spite of hunger and hardship. For the most part people did not seem to know how close they were to the end.

The editor of the *Examiner*, Edward Pollard, writing soon after the war ended, said he was totally surprised when April of 1865 found the fall of Richmond imminent: "The people of Richmond had remained in profound ignorance of the fighting. . . . There was not a rumor of it in the air. Not a newspaper office in the city had any inkling of what was going on."[17] Even John B. Jones, a clerk in the War Department, did not know that Richmond was about to fall. On April 2, 1865, he wrote in his diary: "I hear nothing . . . but the absence of dispatches there is now interpreted as bad news! . . . A decisive struggle is probably at hand. . . . Or there may be nothing in it."[18] Several hours later the long-dreaded news came— Richmond was to be evacuated.

CHAPTER 11

The Fall of Richmond

"This has been an eventful morning," wrote Mrs. William A. Simmons, "while we were at church, in the midst of the service, a messenger came for Pres. Davis, who immediately left the house. An ominous fear fell upon all hearts and seemed to spread itself . . ."[1] Constance Cary "happened to sit in the rear of the President's pew, so near that [she] plainly saw the sort of gray pallor that came upon his face as he read."[2] Jefferson Davis had hoped his leaving the church would not cause any panic. He left quietly and Dr. Minnegerode went on with the Sunday service. However, now he was often interrupted by messengers who came for other government and military officials attending the service at St. Paul's that morning. Finally, Dr. Minnegerode ended the service.

Judith McGuire was attending services at St. James's Church that morning. She had also seen Confederate officials receive messages and leave. At the end of services, she found the streets filled with excited people, "every countenance was wild with excitement . . . we began to understand that the Government was moving, and that the evacuation was indeed going on."[3]

Dr. Moses D. Hoge was conducting services at Second Presbyterian Church when he received a note telling him of the imminent attack on Richmond. He announced the evacuation to his stunned parishioners and then resumed the service.

One eyewitness was most amazed at the shock felt by the people when the news arrived: "Whether or not it was anticipated by the government I do not know; but there can be no doubt that outside of official circles . . . the announcement came with an unexpectedness and surprise of an earthquake."[4] Mary Taylor's diary reflects the same shock. She and her family did not find out about the evacuation order until later in the day. She wrote: "We sauntered slowly homeward, enjoying the calm beauty of the day. After dinner . . . Mr. Ritter came in telling us that Gen'l Lee's lines had been broken in three places at Hatcher's Run and that Richmond would be evacuated in 24 hours. We were stunned and felt that it must be an exaggerated report. . . . The bright sunshine almost seemed a mockery."[5]

President Davis had been advised by General Lee that he could hold on to his position until that night. Davis now gave orders that all critical records and documents must be packed and loaded at the Richmond and Danville Railroad depot by evening and that government officials should leave then also.

Varina Davis and the Davis children had already been sent from the city on Friday. After giving final orders to his Cabinet members, Jefferson Davis returned to the Confederate White House to supervise the packing of his own papers and personal items. For the Confederate officials, plans had long been in place to flee the city safely and quickly. The same was not true for the other residents of Richmond and the day quickly became a scene of chaos.

Sallie Putnam described the scene: "The direful tidings spread with the swiftness of electricity. . . . Thousands of the citizens determined to evacuate the city with the government. . . . The streets were filled with excited crowds hurrying to the different avenues for transportation, intermingled with porters carrying huge loads, and wagons piled up with incongruous heaps of baggage."[6] Judith McGuire wrote of "Baggage-wagons, carts, drays, and ambulances . . . all the indications of alarm and excitement of every kind which could attend such an awful scene."[7]

When night fell, what had already seemed an awful scene to McGuire became much worse. City officials decided to destroy all whiskey supplies and took the barrels out and emptied them into the gutters. A large number of deserting Confederate soldiers discovered the liquor and soon were drunk. Adding to the confusion, many of the guards at the city prisons (not the military prisons where the Union prisoners were held) left their posts. The inmates overwhelmed the remaining guards and escaped to join the looting and drinking in the streets. Sallie Putnam wrote that these were "lawless and desperate villains" and that once they had freed themselves, they "roamed over the city like fierce, ferocious beasts."[8]

Myrta Lockett Avary detailed the vision of the night: "As darkness came upon the city confusion and disorder increased. People were running about everywhere with plunder and provisions . . . . Barrels of liquor were broken open and the gutters ran with whisky and molasses. . . . The air was filled with yells, curses, cries of distress, and horrid songs."[9]

All government storehouses of food and supplies had been opened to the public with the evacuation of the city and the hungry people descended upon the area and "rushed in and secured bacon, clothing, boots" and whatever else they could get.[10] The people were amazed at the amount of food they actually found in the store-

Richmond in flames

houses. For people who literally had been starving, their bitterness at seeing all the hoarded supplies fueled even more rioting and looting. The government decision to destroy all whiskey led to widespread drunkenness. An order came to destroy the tobacco and corn warehouses at 3:00 A.M. and the fire quickly spread to other buildings. Fannie Walker Miller remembered sitting by her window watching "the horrors of that night! The rolling of vehicles, excited cries of the men,

The ruins of a crippled locomotive (left) and Mayo's bridge (below) give some indication of the destruction of part of Richmond.

women, and children as they passed loaded with such goods as they could snatch from the burning factories and stores that were being looted by the frenzied crowds."[11]

The fires continued to spread. Judith McGuire wrote of "being startled by a loud sound like thunder; the house shook and the windows rattled; it seemed like an earthquake in our midst."[12] The magazine where gunpowder was stored had exploded with what Sallie Putnam called the noise "like that of a hundred cannon at one time. The very foundations of the city were shaken."[13] Mary Taylor recorded two explosions: "the most terrific . . . proved to be the blowing up of the powder magazine." The other was "our gun boats at Drury's [Drewry's] Bluff being destroyed."[14]

The decision to "fire" the warehouses of the city was made by General Richard S. Ewell. City officials had begged him not to do this, fearing the consequences if the fires got out of control. But Ewell was determined that nothing be left behind that would be useful to the Union occupiers. The orders included destroying the bridges, military storehouses, tobacco warehouses, and public buildings. LaSalle Corbell Pickett described the flames as "they leaped from house to house in mad revel." When it was all over, she wrote "all the city between Seventh and Fifteenth streets and Main Street and the river was a heap of ashes."[15]

Recorded the *Richmond Daily Whig* on April 4: "For the distance of half a mile from the north side of Main street to the river, and between 8th and 15th streets, embracing upwards of twenty blocks, presents one waste of smoking ruins, blackened walls and broken chimneys."[16]

Kate Mason Rowland wrote: "Such a long, long day! We are no longer in the Confederate lines. . . . The sky in the direction of Richmond is lurid with the glare of burning houses."[17] A large part of the beautiful city of Richmond was no more. And the long-feared destruction had come not from its enemies but from its own government. That would be one of the hardest facts to accept when this bloody struggle finally was over.

CHAPTER 12

Union Soldiers Restore Order

"We took Richmond at 8:15 this morning. I captured many guns. The enemy left in great haste. The city is on fire in two places. Am making every effort to put it out. The people received us with enthusiastic expressions of joy."[1] General Godfrey Weitzel's telegram to Union Secretary of War Edwin Stanton gives a different picture of the surrender of the city than that recorded by the diarists. After reading the newspaper accounts of the general's telegram, Constance Cary wrote to her aunt about a tearful prayer service they had both attended, and then made a sarcastic comment on the general's statement: "Governor Weitzel . . . says in his telegram . . . 'the people received us with the wildest joy.' That scene in Monumental Church looked like it, don't you think so?"[2]

"Exactly at eight o'clock [A.M.] the Confederate flag that fluttered above the Capitol came down and the Stars and Stripes were run up. We knew what that meant! . . . We covered our faces and cried aloud. All through the house was the sound of sobbing. It was as the house of mourning, the house of death."[3] Myrta Lockett Avary's home was not alone in mourning deeply the end of the Confederate capital of Richmond. The most horrible night in their lives behind them, the citizens of Richmond had to face up to their capture and defeat. For many of the poor, including the slaves who now were freed, there was relief and celebration. But for the society ladies there was no

The Stars and Stripes flew over a defeated and ruined Richmond on April 3, 1865.

joy. They had to accept that their world was coming to an end.

Judith McGuire had refused to believe that it could happen for longer than most. In February, she was writing with dismay of the people who "believe that it will be given up . . . it makes me very unhappy." In March she was still strong in her belief: "Oh, I would that I could see Richmond burnt to the ground by its own people, with not one brick left upon another, before its defenceless inhabitants should be subjected to such degradation." The morning of April 3, she saw her ruined city suffering just the humiliation she had feared. In horror, she saw "a regiment of Yankee cavalry come dashing up, yelling, shouting, hallooing, screaming. . . . Then I saw the iron gates of our time-honoured and beautiful Capitol Square . . . thrown open and cavalry dash in. I could see no more; I must go on with a mighty effort, or faint where I stood."[4]

Union troops built a pontoon bridge to cross the James River into Richmond.

The ladies of Richmond were especially horrified that the takeover of the city involved so many black Union soldiers. Mrs. Pryor received a letter from her friend Agnes in Richmond in which she wrote: "At ten o'clock the enemy arrived,—ten thousand negro troops, going on and on, cheered by negroes on the streets."[5] John B. Jones recorded in his diary the feelings of people he spoke to that day: "The white citizens felt annoyed that the city should be held mostly by negro troops. If this measure were not unavoidable, it was impolitic if conciliation be the purpose."[6] For the people of

Richmond, the Union government was giving them the most visible symbol of defeat that was possible.

Some of the arriving Union soldiers found the welcome of the common citizens of Richmond a pleasant one. Charles W. Morrell, a Union soldier, wrote home to his brother from Richmond: "The people brought hundreds of boxes of plug and smoking tobacco and emptied the contents at our feet. In fact the boys wanted for nothing that the people could give us."[7] Another Union man saw more of despair in the welcome of the soldiers by the common people of Richmond: "The people look, many of them at least, ill fed. They are not glad to see Uncle Sam in possession, but they rejoice over the prospect of peace. They resign their hope of independence reluctantly, and are pleased that the day of their privation and endurance is ended. . . . As for Union enthusiasm there is none."[8]

But if the common people of Richmond could put aside their differences and welcome peace, the Union soldiers found another picture among the ladies of Richmond society. Thomas Cooper DeLeon described their reaction this way: "Clad almost invariably in deep mourning—with heavy veils invariably hiding their faces—the broken-hearted daughters of the Capital moved like shadows of the past, through the places that were theirs no longer."[9] Constance Cary wrote that "the town wore the aspect of one in the Middle Ages smitten by pestilence. The streets . . . were empty of the respectable class of inhabitants, the doors and shutters of every house tight closed."[10]

However, the good behavior of the conquering enemy soon won the grudging respect of all the citizens of Richmond, from all levels of society. The *Richmond Daily Whig* of April 4 noted: "The order of the city has been excellent since the occupation by the Federal forces. We have not heard a single complaint on the part of citizens against the soldiers, and we are glad to record that the soldiers have found no reason to complain of the conduct of the citizens. We trust this gratifying state of affairs will continue."[11] F. A. Macartney, writing to his congressman in Maryland, John Cresswell, commented on the behavior of the

Union soldiers: "The troops have behaved splendidly. . . . The townsfolk are amazed especially the women, who believe the stories of brutal outrage and meddlesome insolence told of New Orleans and Savannah. They hardly credit their senses over the order, self respect and courteous deference of our men." [12]

A guard was posted outside the home of General Lee's wife, who had been too ill to leave the city during its evacuation, to protect her and the home's contents. Even Judith McGuire had to admit that "General Ord . . . seems to do every thing in his power to lessen the horrors of this dire calamity." [13] After the smoldering fires were put out with the help of the Union troops, the first need of the city was for food. General Ord appointed General Weitzel as military governor of Richmond, telling him to sell any available tobacco to raise money to feed the poor of the city.

Sallie Putnam wrote: "The evacuation of the city found great numbers of the inhabitants totally without food, and entirely destitute of means by which it might be procured." [14] General Weitzel,

Union General E. O. C. Ord tried to help the starving people of Richmond. He is seen here with his wife and child on the porch of the Confederate White House in Richmond during the occupation.

seeing the terrible need, moved quickly to make food available. Union Secretary of War Stanton was not so willing to help the defeated enemy. He ordered his assistant, Charles A. Dana, to "ascertain from General Weitzel under what authority he is distributing rations to the people of Richmond . . . and direct him to report daily the amount of rations distributed by his order to persons not belonging to the military services, and not authorized by law to receive rations."[15] Dana reported back the next day that Weitzel's orders had come from General Grant and that "He is to pay for rations by selling captured property. Before beginning he is to register the people, and give no one anything who does not take the oath [of allegiance to the United States]."[16]

Sallie Putnam and many others had no choice but starvation. They took the oath and accepted the food given by the hated Yankees. Sallie Putnam couldn't resist, however, describing it this way: "At least one-third of the entire population remaining in the city . . . were driven to the humiliation of subsisting alone on supplies of food furnished them by the conquerors."[17]

CHAPTER 13

Lincoln's Visit and Death

"Mr. Lincoln has visited our devoted city to-day. His reception was any thing but complimentary. Our people were in nothing rude or disrespectful; they only kept themselves away from a scene so painful." Judith McGuire's diary entry continues with her personal feelings on Union President Abraham Lincoln's visit to her childhood home: "I would that dear old house, with all its associations, so sacred to the Southerners, so sweet to us as a family, had shared in the general conflagration [fire]. . . . Oh, how gladly would I have seen it burn!"[1]

Abraham Lincoln arrived in the conquered capital of the Confederate States of America on April 4, 1865. He came in quietly by boat and walked from the dock through the streets of Rich-mond to the home of Jefferson Davis, now the home of the military governor. He spent several hours there, sitting at Jefferson Davis's desk. When Lincoln finished his meetings, he returned to his boat for the trip back to Washington. By then, word had spread and the people of Rich-mond knew he was there. John B. Jones describes the scene as looking "precisely as I had seen royal parties ride in Europe." He also commented on the fact that the cheers for Abraham Lincoln came "mostly from the negroes and Federals."[2]

Sara Pryor's friend Agnes also saw Lincoln that day and wrote her description. Saying she "had a good look at Mr. Lincoln," she describes him as "tired and old—and I must say, with due respect to the President of the United States, I

Freed slaves greeted President Abraham Lincoln when he visited a defeated Richmond on April 4, 1865.

thought him the ugliest man I had ever seen."[3]

Abraham Lincoln was not the only Northerner to visit the captured city. One writer described hundreds of them "flocking" to Richmond to see the ruins of this great city. For the women of Richmond, these visiting Northerners, and especially Abraham Lincoln, brought nothing but pain and anger. Phoebe Pember wrote bitterly of "the arrival of former friends, sometimes people moving in the best classes of society, who had the bad taste to make a pleasure trip to the mourning city, calling upon their heart-broken friends of happier days in all the finery of the newest New York fashions."[4] Mary Taylor wrote disgustedly of two visiting Yankee soldiers who told her "we would all soon be under the old flag, and would *love* each other."[5]

In many ways, the ladies of the Confederate capital had not really surrendered, in spite of the Union occupation of their city. Phoebe Pember described the mood of the city: "There were few men in the city at this time; but the women of the South still fought their battle for them: fought it resentfully, calmly, but silently! Clad in their mourning garments, overcome but hardly subdued, they sat within their desolate homes. . . . By no sign or act did the possessors of their fair city know that they were even conscious of their presence . . . they [Union soldiers] might have supposed themselves a phantom army."[6]

The anger of the city residents reached its peak when they heard of the order by General Weitzel that prayers must be offered for Abraham Lincoln during church services on Sunday, April 9. When the city of Atlanta had fallen in 1864, a similar order had been given to the religious leaders of that city. DeLeon wrote that the result in Atlanta was that "the public worship ceased, and all services were held in private homes until the Washington government rescinded the [General] Thomas order."[7] Now the same demand of prayers for the President was being made of the fallen capital of the Confederacy. Judith McGuire, a minister's wife, and more charitable in her writing than most of the diarists, reacted with disgust: "Is the Church to pray for the Northern President? How is it possible, except as we pray for all other sinners?"[8]

Actually, General Weitzel did not direct that prayers be offered for President Lincoln. His order had given permission for church services on the general condition that no disloyal sentiments should be uttered. His reasonable approach got him in trouble with his superiors. Secretary of War Stanton, already angry about the decision to feed the starving Richmond residents, censured Weitzel strongly for allowing "such an omission of respect to the President of the United States."[9] Weitzel reported to Stanton's assistant, Charles Dana, that he had specifically avoided mentioning the prayer for the Union president as a "result of the President's verbal direction to him, to let them down easy."[10] Secretary of War Stanton would not accept this explanation. The dispute over the prayer for the President would probably have continued for some time, but the assassination of Abraham Lincoln ended that discussion.

For all their dislike of Abraham Lincoln, Confederate women did not wish him dead. They reacted with horror to the news of Lincoln's assassination at Ford's Theatre. They knew that this meant for them an end to any gracious peace the North might offer. On April 17, 1865, the *Richmond Daily Whig* announced that Lincoln had died on April 15: "The heaviest blow which has ever fallen upon the people of the South has descended. Abraham Lincoln, the President of the United States, has been assassinated . . . every reflecting person will deplore the awful event."[11] Union soldier Charles W. Morrell wrote home to his brother from Richmond on April 17, 1865: "I think the masses of the Southern people will deeply sympathize with the people of the North in the Nation's loss."[12]

Mary Boykin Chesnut received a secret dispatch for her husband and opened it, as he was away. The news shocked her: "I sent off messenger after messenger for General Chesnut. I have not the faintest idea where he is, but I know this foul murder will bring upon us worse miseries."[13] Lt. John S. Wise, traveling with what still remained of the Confederate Army of Tennessee, wrote of the reaction to the news in camp: "Among the higher officers and the most intelligent and conservative men, the assassination caused a shudder of horror at the heinousness of the act, and at the thought of its possible consequences; but among the thoughtless, the desperate, and the ignorant, it was hailed as a sort of retributive justice. . . . To us, Lincoln was an inhuman monster."[14]

Lincoln (1809-1865) was shot on April 14, 1865, and died the next day. His body lay in state in the Capitol and was then taken by train (shown here) to Springfield, Illinois, for burial on May 4.

Judith McGuire saw in Abraham Lincoln's death a fulfillment of "the warnings of Scripture. His efforts . . . have caused the shedding of oceans of Southern blood, and by man it now seems has his blood been shed." [15] But, with others, she also knew that the death of Lincoln would bring nothing but trouble for the South. Cornelia Peake McDonald, widowed just four and a half months before the Civil War ended, shared McGuire's mixed feelings: "When I first heard of the taking off of Lincoln, I thought it was just what he deserved; he that had urged on and promoted a savage war that had cost so many lives; but a little reflection made me see that it was worse for us than if he had been suffered to live for . . . he was disposed to be merciful." [16]

Thomas Cooper DeLeon, writing years later, having lived through the Reconstruction Period in the South, believed that "the madman Booth's pistol" had "jarred apart the closing wound of war-born hatred." He felt that Lincoln would have been merciful to the defeated South if he had lived. [17]

William Asbury Christian, also writing years later, held the same view: "Even those of the most ultra Southern feelings believed that Lincoln had planned for a speedy and liberal settlement of the existing difficulties in Virginia." The people of Richmond, he wrote, were "appalled." They had suffered a "deplorable calamity" and "on every hand were expressions of regret and abhorrence." [18]

Just a short time after reacting with horror to the thought of even praying for President Lincoln, the people of Richmond mourned his loss and theirs.

CHAPTER 14

Richmond at the End

The Confederate ladies showed a devotion to all of their generals, but most especially to General Lee. Late in 1862, Mrs. General Lee (as she was often referred to in the South) received a letter from a woman who was "making an effort to procure the hair of as many Confederate Generals, prominent in our now pending revolution, as practicable, to make a wreath of flowers which may in future years, be cherished as a national relick."[1] Hair was often used at the time to make jewelry for family members. A number of hair wreaths and bracelets can be found in museums.

During the Civil War, many women decided to collect the hair of famous people to use in making "memory" jewelry. Mrs. Lee sent her a lock of the general's hair and then proceeded to help the woman to collect the hair of others who visited her while in Richmond. The love and admiration of these women for the general was boundless. There would be much discussion in the South later on as to why the South lost the war. Many people would be blamed, but never Robert E. Lee. He remained the South's hero to the very end.

"General Lee has returned. He came unattended, save by his staff—came without notice, and without parade; but he could not come unobserved," wrote Judith McGuire on April 17, 1865, of Robert E. Lee's return to his home on Franklin Street.[2] He had returned after surrendering to Union General Ulysses S. Grant at Appomattox Court House, Virginia, on Palm Sunday, April 9.

Jewelry made of hair, such as this necklace, was popular in the South during the Civil War. Often the hair came from relatives who were soldiers or from famous people.

Sallie Putnam also saw him arrive and remarked on the crowds, "As he dismounted from his horse, large numbers pressed around him, and shook his hand warmly and sympathetically."[3]

Myrta Lockett Avary noticed most how tired he seemed to be as "he bared his weary gray head to the people who gathered around him with greetings."[4] Judith McGuire, as a friend of Mrs. Lee's, had often seen the general when he was in Richmond for meetings. She had often noted what the war was doing to her friend: "His beard is very long," she wrote in 1863, "and painfully gray, which makes him appear much older than he really is."[5] Now, as she welcomed home her old friend, she wrote of him in her diary her highest tribute: "He has returned from defeat and disaster with the universal and profound admiration of the world, having done all that skill and valour could accomplish."[6]

Thomas DeLeon wrote that Robert E. Lee "simply bowing his head, . . . passed silently to his own door; it closed upon him, and his people had seen him for the last time in his battle harness."[7]

The return of Lee finally brought home to the citizens of Richmond the fact that the fight was indeed over. Lee himself signaled this by giving away buttons and stars from his uniforms to the young girls who came asking for them. Louise Triplett Harrison was away at the time. Upon returning to Richmond, she went to visit her friend, the general's daughter, Mildred. "The general," she wrote "asked if I would go with him into his little office. Out of one of the little old trunks he had carried through the war, he took a button and a star which he said he had saved for me, thinking I would care to have them."[8]

It really was all over. All the deaths of Confederate soldiers had not served to bring success to their Cause. All the sacrifice and suffering and devotion of the women of the South who had worked harder than anyone would have believed possible, had not saved the Confederacy. The social structure of Richmond was destroyed. Many of its wealthiest and most prominent citizens had lost everything for the Cause. Mary Boykin Chesnut arrived at her plantation to find "every window had been broken, every bell torn down, every piece of furniture destroyed, and every door smashed in. . . . When we crossed the river coming home, the ferry man at Chesnut's Ferry asked for his fee. Among us all we could not muster the small silver coin he demanded."[9] Others had profited in blockade running and earned the hatred of those who had previously been friends.

It had been a doomed struggle from the beginning. The North had more material, more money, and more manpower to fight this war. The successful blockade of Southern ports by the Union Navy and the refusal of the European nations to enter the war on the South's side doomed any chance the Confederacy might have had to overcome the odds. The South had many of the best generals, particularly at the beginning of the conflict, but that only prolonged the length and devastation of the war. The Southern social leadership truly believed that "One Southern man is equal to three Yankees."[10] They allowed this belief to bring about their own ruin. The South felt themselves to be superior to the North and just could not imagine defeat.

The story told in the diaries is a powerful one. It is the story of a people who were truly willing to give up everything for their Cause. Reading their accounts, knowing that defeat was coming, is a very saddening experience. History shows that they really did give up everything—their sons, brothers, and husbands died in terrible numbers. Their fortunes were gone. Their way of life was destroyed.

Had it all been worth the effort and the cost? Let us give the last word to Judith McGuire. "How all this happened—how Grant's hundreds of thousands overcame our little band, history, not I, must tell my children's children. It is enough for me to tell them that all that bravery and self-denial could do has been done."[11]

SOURCE NOTES

Prologue

1. Mrs. Burton Harrison [Constance Cary], *Recollections, Grave and Gay* (New York: Charles Scribner's Sons, 1911), pp. 201–202.
2. Judith W. McGuire, *Diary of a Southern Refugee during the War* (New York: E. J. Hale & Son, 1867), p. 341.
3. Harrison, p. 202.
4. *Richmond Daily Whig*, Richmond, Virginia, February 11, 1865.
5. Harrison, pp. 204–205.
6. McGuire, p. 341.
7. Harrison, p. 203.

Chapter 1

1. Virginia Tunstall Clay-Clopton, *A Belle of the Fifties* (New York: Doubleday, Page & Company, 1905), p. 168.
2. William Asbury Christian, *Richmond, her past and present* (Richmond: L. H. Jenkins, 1912), pp. 207–208.
3. Clay, p. 142.
4. Clay, p. 147.
5. Jefferson Davis, *Inaugural Address* as contained in Varina Davis, *Jefferson Davis: A Memoir by his wife* (New York: Belford Co., 1890), Vol. II, p. 24.
6. Sarah [Sallie] A. Brock Putnam, *Richmond During the War* (New York: G. W. Carleton & Company, 1867), pp. 17, 22.
7. Judith W. McGuire, *Diary of a Southern Refugee during the War* (New York: E. J. Hale & Son, 1867), pp. 16–17.

8. Kate Mason Rowland, Diary, January 21, 1861, (Extract from a letter of Emily Mason). Eleanor S. Brockenbrough Library, The Museum of the Confederacy, Richmond, Virginia.
9. Phoebe Yates Pember, *A Southern Woman's Story* (New York: G.W. Carleton & Company, 1879), p. 13.
10. McGuire, pp. 21–22.
11. McGuire, p. 26.
12. Myrta Lockett Avary, *A Virginia Girl in the Civil War* (New York: D. Appleton and Company, 1903), p. 23–24.
13. Putnam, p. 27.

Chapter 2

1. Sarah [Sallie] A. Brock Putnam, *Richmond During the War* (New York: G. W. Carleton & Company, 1867), p. 76.
2. Judith W. McGuire, *Diary of a Southern Refugee during the War* (New York: E. J. Hale & Son, 1867), p. 96.
3. Varina Davis, *Jefferson Davis: A Memoir by his wife* (New York: Belford Co., 1890), Vol. II, pp. 200–203.
4. Putnam, p. 78.
5. McGuire, p. 88.

Chapter 3

1. Fannie A. Beers, *Memories: A Record of Personal Experience and Adventure during four years of war* (Philadelphia: J.B. Lippincott Company, 1889), p. 27.
2. Mary Boykin Chesnut, *A Diary from Dixie* (New York: D. Appleton and Company, 1905), p. 69.

3. *Richmond Daily Whig*, Richmond, Virginia, May 22, 1861.
4. *Examiner*, Richmond, Virginia, November 18, 1861.
5. Chesnut, p. 96.
6. William Asbury Christian, *Richmond, her past and present* (Richmond: L. H. Jenkins, 1912), p. 220.
7. Judith W. McGuire, *Diary of a Southern Refugee during the War* (New York: E. J. Hale & Son, 1867), p. 26.
8. Sara Agnes (Rice) Pryor, *Reminiscences of Peace and War* (New York: Macmillan Company, 1905), p. 135.
9. Pryor, p. 131.
10. McGuire, p. 26.
11. Ellen Mordecai, Letter to Brother, June 6, 1861. Alfred Mordecai Papers, Manuscript Division, Library of Congress.
12. Varina Davis, *Jefferson Davis: A Memoir by his wife* (New York: Belford Co., 1890), Vol. II, p. 209.
13. Sarah [Sallie] A. Brock Putnam, *Richmond During the War* (New York: G. W. Carleton & Company, 1867), p. 39.
14. Thomas Cooper DeLeon, *Belles, beaux, and brains of the 60's* (New York: G.W. Dillingham Company, 1907), pp. 136–137.
15. *Richmond Daily Whig*. Richmond, Virginia, July 6, 1864.
16. Douglas Southall Freeman, "When War Came to Richmond," *Richmond News Leader*, September 8, 1937 (Special Bicentennial Issue), p. 78.
17. Mary Boykin Chesnut, *A Diary from Dixie*, ed. by Ben Ames Williams (Boston: Houghton Mifflin Company, 1949), p. 75.
18. *Examiner*, Richmond, Virginia, June 28, 1861, p. 3; August 27, 1861, p. 3; September 16, 1861, p. 3; October 8, 1861, p. 3; November 11, 1861, p. 3.
19. Thomas Cooper DeLeon, *Four Years in Rebel Capitals* (Mobile, Alabama: The Gossip Printing Co., 1890), p. 238.
20. DeLeon, *Belles*, pp. 367–368.
21. Putnam, p. 42.

Chapter 4

1. *Examiner*, Richmond, Virginia, July 22, 1861.
2. Fannie A. Beers, *Memories: A Record of Personal Experience and Adventure during four years of war* (Philadelphia: J.B. Lippincott Company, 1889), p. 25.
3. Mary Boykin Chesnut, *A Diary from Dixie* (New York: D. Appleton and Company, 1905), pp. 86–88.
4. Sarah [Sallie] A. Brock Putnam, *Richmond During the War* (New York: G. W. Carleton & Company, 1867), p. 65.
5. *Richmond Daily Whig*, Richmond, Virginia, July 24, 1861, p. 3.
6. Putnam, pp. 65–66.
7. Phoebe Yates Pember, *A Southern Woman's Story* (New York: G.W. Carleton & Company, 1879), p. 122.
8. Chesnut, p. 107.
9. Judith W. McGuire, *Diary of a Southern Refugee during the War* (New York: E. J. Hale & Son, 1867), p. 43.

Chapter 5

1. *Examiner*, Richmond, Virginia, June 1, 1861.
2. *Richmond Daily Whig*, Richmond, Virginia, May 18, 1861.
3. Mrs. Burton Harrison [Constance Cary], *Recollections, Grave and Gay* (New York: Charles Scribner's Sons, 1911), p. 58.
4. Thomas Cooper DeLeon, *Belles, beaux, and brains of the 60's* (New York: G.W. Dillingham Company, 1907), p. 412.
5. Harrison, p. 146.
6. Sarah [Sallie] A. Brock Putnam, *Richmond During the War* (New York: G. W. Carleton & Company, 1867), p. 33.
7. Thomas Cooper DeLeon, *Four Years in Rebel Capitals* (Mobile, Alabama: The Gossip Printing Co., 1890), pp. 148–149.
8. DeLeon, *Belles*, p. 62.
9. Harrison, p. 61.

10. Putnam, p. 78.
11. Putnam, pp. 104–105.
12. Catherine C. Hopley, *Life in the South* (London: Chapman and Hall, 1863), p. 40.
13. Putnam, p. 114.
14. Virginia Tunstall Clay-Clopton, *A Belle of the Fifties* (New York: Doubleday, Page & Company, 1905), p. 169.
15. Clay, p. 178.

Chapter 6

1. John Beauchamp Jones, *A Rebel War Clerk's Diary* (Philadelphia: J. B. Lippincott, 1866), Vol. I, p. 138.
2. Sara Agnes (Rice) Pryor, *Reminiscences of Peace and War* (New York: Macmillan Company, 1905), p. 178.
3. Thomas Cooper DeLeon, *Four Years in Rebel Capitals* (Mobile, Alabama: The Gossip Printing Co., 1890), p. 198.
4. Judith W. McGuire, *Diary of a Southern Refugee during the War* (New York: E. J. Hale & Son, 1867), p. 107.
5. Sarah [Sallie] A. Brock Putnam, *Richmond During the War* (New York: G. W. Carleton & Company, 1867), p. 129.
6. *War of the Rebellion: A Compilation of the Official Records of the Union and Confederate Armies.* Washington, D.C.: Government Printing Office, 1890–1901, Series I Vol. XI, p. 504.
7. McGuire, p. 110.
8. Mrs. Burton Harrison [Constance Cary], *Recollections, Grave and Gay* (New York: Charles Scribner's Sons, 1911), p. 82.
9. LaSalle Corbell Pickett, *Pickett and his Men* (Atlanta: Foote & Davies Company, 1899), p. 173.
10. McGuire, pp. 125–126.
11. Pickett, pp. 173–174.
12. McGuire, p. 126.

13. Harrison, p. 84.
14. Putnam, p. 149.
15. Pickett, p. 174.

Chapter 7

1. Fannie A. Beers, *Memories: A Record of Personal Experience and Adventure during four years of war* (Philadelphia: J. B. Lippincott Company, 1889), p. 46.
2. Louisa Triplett Harrison, "Letter to Thomas DeLeon," quoted in Thomas Cooper DeLeon, *Belles, beaux, and brains of the 60's* (New York: G.W. Dillingham Company, 1907), p. 127.
3. Thomas Cooper DeLeon, *Belles, beaux, and brains of the 60's.* (New York: G.W. Dillingham Company,) 1907, p. 389.
4. C. Vann Woodward, ed. *Mary Chesnut's Civil War* (New Haven: Yale University Press, 1981), p. 133.
5. Phoebe Yates Pember, *A Southern Woman's Story* (New York: G.W. Carleton & Company, 1879), p. 138.
6. Pember, p. 75.
7. Varina Davis, *Jefferson Davis: A Memoir by his wife* (New York: Belford Co., 1890), Vol. II, pp. 204, 206.
8. Sara Agnes (Rice) Pryor, *Reminiscences of Peace and War* (New York: Macmillan Company, 1905), p. 171.
9. Judith W. McGuire, *Diary of a Southern Refugee during the War* (New York: E. J. Hale & Son, 1867), pp. 29–30.
10. McGuire, p. 177.

Chapter 8

1. John Beauchamp Jones, *A Rebel War Clerk's Diary* (Philadelphia: J. B. Lippincott, 1866), Vol. I, p. 165.
2. Sara Agnes (Rice) Pryor, *Reminiscences of Peace and War* (New York: Macmillan Company, 1905), p. 253.

3. Sarah [Sallie] A. Brock Putnam, *Richmond During the War* (New York: G. W. Carleton & Company, 1867), p. 80.
4. Pryor, p. 221.
5. Mrs. Mark Valentine, "A Girl in the Sixties in Richmond," *Confederate Veteran*, Vol. XX (1912), p. 279.
6. Jones, Vol. II, p. 16.
7. Judith W. McGuire, *Diary of a Southern Refugee during the War* (New York: E. J. Hale & Son, 1867), pp. 235, 225.
8. Putnam, p. 194.
9. Putnam, pp. 189–190.
10. William Asbury Christian, *Richmond, her past and present* (Richmond: L. H. Jenkins, 1912), p. 240.
11. McGuire, p. 202.
12. *War of the Rebellion: A Compilation of the Official Records of the Union and Confederate Armies.* Washington, D.C.: Government Printing Office, 1890–1901, Series I Vol. XVIII, p. 958.
13. Varina Davis, *Jefferson Davis: A Memoir by his wife* (New York: Belford Co., 1890), Vol. II, p. 374.
14. Putnam, p. 209.
15. Kate Mason Rowland, Diary, April 4, 1863. Eleanor S. Brockenbrough Library, The Museum of the Confederacy, Richmond, Virginia.
16. McGuire, p. 203.
17. Pryor, p. 238.
18. McGuire, p. 203.

Chapter 9

1. Judith W. McGuire, *Diary of a Southern Refugee during the War* (New York: E. J. Hale & Son, 1867), pp. 211–212.
2. McGuire, p. 212.
3. Kate Mason Rowland, Diary, May 12, 1863. Eleanor S. Brockenbrough Library, The Museum of the Confederacy, Richmond, Virginia.
4. *Examiner*, Richmond, Virginia, May 12, 1863.
5. Sarah [Sallie] A. Brock Putnam, *Richmond During the War* (New York: G. W. Carleton & Company, 1867), p. 219.

6. Sara Agnes (Rice) Pryor, *Reminiscences of Peace and War* (New York: Macmillan Company, 1905), p. 243.
7. McGuire, p. 262.
8. Mrs. Burton Harrison [Constance Cary], *Recollections, Grave and Gay* (New York: Charles Scribner's Sons, 1911), p. 182.
9. *Examiner*, Richmond, Virginia, May 14, 1864.
10. McGuire, p. 267.
11. Cornelia Peake McDonald, *A Woman's Civil War* (Madison: University of Wisconsin, 1992), pp. 215–216.
12. McGuire, p. 230.
13. Mary Boykin Chesnut, *A Diary from Dixie* (New York: D. Appleton and Company, 1905), pp. 214–215.
14. William Asbury Christian, *Richmond, her past and present* (Richmond: L. H. Jenkins, 1912), p. 231.
15. *Richmond Daily Dispatch*, Richmond, Virginia, July 4, 1863.
16. Harrison, p. 83.

Chapter 10

1. Virginia Tunstall Clay-Clopton, *A Belle of the Fifties* (New York: Doubleday, Page & Company, 1905), p. 222.
2. Sara Agnes (Rice) Pryor, *Reminiscences of Peace and War* (New York: Macmillan Company, 1905), p. 327.
3. John Beauchamp Jones, *A Rebel War Clerk's Diary* (Philadelphia: J. B. Lippincott, 1866), Vol. II, p. 173.
4. Mrs. Mark Valentine, "A Girl in the Sixties in Richmond," *Confederate Veteran*, Vol. XX (June 1912), p. 280.
5. Sarah [Sallie] A. Brock Putnam, *Richmond During the War* (New York: G. W. Carleton & Company, 1867), p. 303.
6. Judith W. McGuire, *Diary of a Southern Refugee during the War* (New York: E. J. Hale & Son, 1867), pp. 257, 292.
7. William Asbury Christian, *Richmond, her past and present* (Richmond: L. H. Jenkins, 1912), p. 254.
8. Jones, Vol. II, p. 458.
9. Jones, Vol. II, p. 135.

10. McGuire, p. 251.
11. Clay, pp. 223-227.
12. Myrta Lockett Avary, *A Virginia Girl in the Civil War* (New York: D. Appleton and Company, 1903), pp. 336, 353.
13. McGuire, p. 328.
14. Pryor, pp. 226–227.
15. John S. Wise, *The End of an Era* (Boston: Houghton, Mifflin and Company, 1901), p. 397.
16. Mrs. Burton Harrison [Constance Cary], *Recollections, Grave and Gay* (New York: Charles Scribner's Sons, 1911), p. 150.
17. Edward A. Pollard, *The Lost Cause* (New York: E. B. Treat & Company, 1867), p. 693.
18. Jones, Vol. II, p. 465.

Chapter 11

1. Mrs. Wm. A. Simmons, "The Flight from Richmond." Southern Women's History Collection. Eleanor S. Brockenbrough Library, The Museum of the Confederacy, Richmond, Virginia.
2. Mrs. Burton Harrison [Constance Cary], *Recollections, Grave and Gay* (New York: Charles Scribner's Sons, 1911), p. 207.
3. Judith W. McGuire, *Diary of a Southern Refugee during the War* (New York: E. J. Hale & Son, 1867), pp. 343–344.
4. Reprint of an article in the *Richmond Daily Dispatch*, February 3, 1902. *Southern Historical Society Papers*, Vol. XXIX, p. 152.
5. Mary Taylor, 1865 Diary, April 2, 1865. Charles Elisha Taylor Papers (#3091), Special Collections Department, University of Virginia Library.
6. Sarah [Sallie] A. Brock Putnam, *Richmond During the War* (New York: G. W. Carleton & Company, 1867), p. 363.
7. McGuire, p. 344.
8. Putnam, p. 364.
9. Myrta Lockett Avary, *A Virginia Girl in the Civil War* (New York: D. Appleton and Company, 1903), pp. 360–361.

10. *Evening Whig*, Richmond, Virginia, April 4, 1865.
11. Fannie Walker Miller, "The Fall of Richmond," *Confederate Veteran.* Vol. XIII (1905), p. 305.
12. McGuire, p. 345.
13. Putnam, p. 365.
14. Taylor, April 3, 1865.
15. LaSalle Corbell Pickett, *Pickett and his Men* (Atlanta: Foote & Davies Company, 1899), p. 2.
16. *Richmond Daily Whig*, Richmond, Virginia, April 4, 1865.
17. Kate Mason Rowland, Diary, April 3, 1865. Eleanor S. Brockenbrough Library, The Museum of the Confederacy, Richmond, Virginia.

Chapter 12

1. *War of the Rebellion: A Compilation of the Official Records of the Union and Confederate Armies.* Washington, D.C.: Government Printing Office, 1890–1901, Series I Vol. XLVI, p. 509.
2. Mrs. Burton Harrison [Constance Cary], *Recollections, Grave and Gay* (New York: Charles Scribner's Sons, 1911), p. 216.
3. Myrta Lockett Avary, *A Virginia Girl in the Civil War* (New York: D. Appleton and Company, 1903), p. 362.
4. Judith W. McGuire, *Diary of a Southern Refugee during the War* (New York: E. J. Hale & Son, 1867), pp. 332, 340, 346.
5. Sara Agnes (Rice) Pryor, *Reminiscences of Peace and War* (New York: Macmillan Company, 1905), p. 356.
6. John Beauchamp Jones, *A Rebel War Clerk's Diary* (Philadelphia: J. B. Lippincott, 1866), Vol. II, p. 471.
7. Charles W. Morrell, Letters. April 13, 1865. Manuscript Division, Library of Congress.
8. F. A. Macartney, Letter. April 11, 1865. John Angel James Cresswell Papers, Manuscript Division, Library of Congress.
9. Thomas Cooper DeLeon, *Four Years in Rebel Capitals* (Mobile, Alabama: The Gossip Printing Co., 1890), p. 363.

10. Harrison, p. 212.
11. *Richmond Daily Whig*, Richmond, Virginia, April 4, 1865.
12. Macartney, Letter.
13. McGuire, p. 349.
14. Sarah [Sallie] A. Brock Putnam, *Richmond During the War* (New York: G. W. Carleton & Company, 1867), p. 372.
15. *War of the Rebellion*, p. 594.
16. *War of the Rebellion*, p. 619.
17. Putnam, p. 373.

Chapter 13

1. Judith W. McGuire, *Diary of a Southern Refugee during the War* (New York: E. J. Hale & Son, 1867), p. 350.
2. John Beauchamp Jones, *A Rebel War Clerk's Diary* (Philadelphia: J. B. Lippincott, 1866), Vol. II, pp. 470–471.
3. Sara Agnes (Rice) Pryor, *Reminiscences of Peace and War* (New York: Macmillan Company, 1905), p. 357.
4. Phoebe Yates Pember, *A Southern Woman's Story* (New York: G.W. Carleton & Company, 1879), p. 177.
5. Mary Taylor, 1865 Diary, April 3, 1865. Charles Elisha Taylor Papers (#3091), Special Collections Department, University of Virginia Library.
6. Pember, pp. 176–177.
7. Thomas Cooper DeLeon, *Belles, beaux, and brains of the 60's* (New York: G.W. Dillingham Company, 1907), p. 375.
8. McGuire, pp. 349–350.
9. *War of the Rebellion: A Compilation of the Official Records of the Union and Confederate Armies.* Washington, D.C.: Government Printing Office, 1890–1901, Series I Vol. XLVI, p.678.
10. *War of the Rebellion*, p. 684.
11. *Richmond Daily Whig*, Richmond, Virginia, April 17, 1865.
12. Charles W. Morrell, Letters. April 13, 1865. Manuscript Division, Library of Congress.

13. Mary Boykin Chesnut, *A Diary from Dixie* (New York: D. Appleton and Company, 1905), p. 380.
14. John S. Wise, *The End of an Era* (Boston: Houghton, Mifflin and Company, 1901), pp. 454–455.
15. McGuire, p. 356.
16. Cornelia Peake McDonald, *A Woman's Civil War* (Madison: University of Wisconsin, 1992), p. 235.
17. DeLeon, p. 455.
18. William Asbury Christian, *Richmond, her past and present* (Richmond: L. H. Jenkins, 1912), p. 268.

Chapter 14

1. J. E. Conrad, Letter, December 25, 1862. Robert E. Lee Family Collection. Eleanor S. Brockenbrough Library, The Museum of the Confederacy, Richmond, Virginia.
2. Judith W. McGuire, *Diary of a Southern Refugee during the War* (New York: E. J. Hale & Son, 1867), p. 356.
3. Sarah [Sallie] A. Brock Putnam, *Richmond During the War* (New York: G. W. Carleton & Company, 1867), p. 379.
4. Myrta Lockett Avary, *A Virginia Girl in the Civil War* (New York: D. Appleton and Company, 1903), p. 373.
5. McGuire, p. 214.
6. McGuire, p. 356.
7. Thomas Cooper DeLeon, *Four Years in Rebel Capitals* (Mobile, Alabama: The Gossip Printing Co., 1890), p. 367.
8. Louisa Triplett Harrison, "Letter to Thomas DeLeon," quoted in Thomas Cooper DeLeon, *Belles, beaux, and brains of the 60's* (New York: G.W. Dillingham Company, 1907), pp. 419–420.
9. Mary Boykin Chesnut, *A Diary from Dixie* (New York: D. Appleton and Company, 1905), pp. 386–388.
10. McGuire, p. 38.
11. McGuire, p. 353.

FOR FURTHER INFORMATION

Books

Beller, Susan Provost. *Medical Practices in the Civil War.* Charlotte, VT: OurStory, 1992.

Blashfield, Jean R. *Women at the Front: Their Changing Roles in the Civil War.* Danbury, CT: Franklin Watts, 1997.

Chang, Ina. *A Separate Battle: Women and the Civil War.* New York: Lodestar, 1991.

Damon, Duane. *When this Cruel War is Over: The Civil War Home Front.* Minneapolis: Lerner, 1996.

Emert, Phyllis Raybin. *Women in the Civil War: Warriors, Patriots, Nurses and Spies.* Carlisle, MA: Discovery Enterprises, 1994.

Gay, Kathlyn. *The Civil War.* Voices from the Past. New York: Twenty-First Century Books, 1995.

Ray, Delia. *A Nation Torn: The Story of How the Civil War Began.* New York: Puffin Books, 1996.

Shura, Mary Frances. *Gentle Annie: The True Story of a Civil War Nurse.* New York: Scholastic, 1994.

Sigerman, Harriet. *An Unfinished Battle: American Women 1848–1865.* New York: Oxford University Press, 1994.

Zeinert, Karen. *Those Courageous Women of the Civil War.* Brookfield, CT: The Millbrook Press, 1998.

CD-Rom

American Heritage. *The Civil War: The Complete Multimedia Experience.* Simon & Schuster Interactive, 1995.

Internet Resources

Civil War Women: Primary Sources on the Internet. Duke University.
http://scriptorium.lib.duke.edu/women/cwdocs.html

Library of Congress Civil War Photographs (1,118 photographs)
http://lcweb2.loc.gov/cwphome.html

Museum of the Confederacy Women's Exhibit
http://www.moc.org/womanwar.htm

National Archives Pictures of the Civil War
http://gopher.nara.gov:70/Oh/inform/dc/audvis/still/civwar.html

National Park Service Links to the Past
http://www.cr.nps.gov/colherit.htm

INDEX

Page numbers in *italics* refer to illustrations.